Messages from Beyond the Veil

SPIRITUAL GUIDANCE FOR OUR HUMAN EXPERIENCE

REGINALD H. GRAY

DAVID J. DYE

Astralis

MEDIA GROUP, LLC

Gilbert, Arizona

Published in partnership with Celestial Publishers, L.L.C.

www.MessagesFromBeyondTheVeil.com

ISBN: 0692842098
ISBN-13: 978-0692842096

DEDICATION

Reginald Gray

To my wife, Helen, for her unstinting efforts in transcribing and whose unwavering support was invaluable in seeing this work come to fruition. Our mutual journey on the path has illustrated to me the reality of soulmates. She and our sons have been a true motivation for me to share the principles in this book by which we have attempted to live our lives.

David Dye

To my parents, Marsha and Harvey. They instilled in me at a very young age a grand wonder about the nature of the Universe and our purpose for existence, a love of science and science-fiction, and the belief that anything is possible.

CONTENTS

FOREWORD

The first time I heard my colleague David Dye read an excerpt from the book you are now holding, I had an incredible experience of déjà vu. How could I relate so powerfully to the story of a group of people who were regularly meeting behind closed doors to explore spiritual truths? Perhaps it is that I am a Seeker in this lifetime and very likely have been in many lifetimes before.

For many, understanding spirituality is a lifelong journey of seeking. There is something deep within us that yearns to know what is beyond our comprehension; we crave answers to esoteric and mystical questions that cannot be satisfied by conventional wisdom.

These messages, which were passed down to humanity at a time when the world was seeing the opening blows of a horrific war that resulted in tens of millions of casualties, cover some of the deepest questions of the mortal and heavenly realms—questions Seekers have been asking throughout the millennia.

It is appropriate then that *Messages from Beyond the Veil* is being released now—at a time which is perhaps not so dissimilar from the days when that group of dedicated individuals gathered together to seek wisdom from the other side. We are now, more than ever, observing the consequences of losing sight of our Oneness. Knowing this, it is beautiful and critical to have the counsel offered within these pages—to remind us once more of the necessity of love and of our own inherent goodness.

Blessings on your journey of discovery and illumination as you read the timeless messages within this work.

KC Miller
Founder of Southwest Institute of Healing Arts

PREFACE

In the early 1930s, a group of men and women had been meeting regularly in London to discuss spiritual matters and to meditate on life and its meaning. Those were dark days for Europe as civil unrest was spreading in Germany and neighboring countries. The Depression was destroying hope with savage efficiency, and horrifying memories of the butchery and carnage of the Great War were still vivid. Several in the gathering had witnessed firsthand the results of mankind's inhumanity and the depths to which those in power were capable of descending. Was humanity doomed to repeat the senseless brutality of the World War? Was there no alternative to the hate and vitriol that seemed to define the times?

While meditating one night, an individual in the group who was particularly spiritually sensitive felt as if someone was trying to get her attention; however, it was not one of the other participants in the meeting. This was the first contact from the messengers. As she began to realize that she was channeling an entity from another realm, she also became clear that the spiritual being was urging her to record its words. Thus, the group began the process of detailing these communications.

Several years later, all-out war was taking shape across Europe, and yet, the group persevered. They continued their sessions until the bombing of London by Nazi Germany effectively ended the possibility of further meetings. Some sought shelter and others were dispersed in the defense of Britain.

While in refuge, one of the members in the group befriended my grandfather and entrusted him to protect the transcripts and notes, which he did when he emigrated to the United States.

I was completely unaware of the transcripts' existence until the fateful day my grandfather called me into his bedroom. He wanted me to have them because he did not want me to grieve his imminent death. The messages, he told me, would explain our true origin and purpose as humans on Earth and give me reason to rejoice in his "transition," as he refused to call it death. My grandfather suggested that I publish the messages, as that was the original purpose of the spirits in establishing contact—that humanity may benefit from the truths revealed. More than thirty years have passed since that day, and the wishes of my grandfather have at last been fulfilled.

iii

In this work you will read the original passages denoted in italics as they were recorded more than eighty years ago, including their concept of spelling. The book follows the chronology with which the messages were recorded. You will notice the information becomes more detailed and descriptive as you advance into the material. Per the group's notes, the spirit entities initially had difficulty in conveying celestial "thoughts" and the receivers struggled to put them into the written word. As time passed, they became more adept at bridging the gap between the two worlds.

The commentary interspersed between the messages is a combination of our writing and the group's notes. Our impressions reflect our study of metaphysics, parapsychology, and spiritual writings over many years.

Are the messages genuine? Do they come from the heavenly realms? This you must decide for yourself. David and I have no doubt in their authenticity. The truths to be found in this volume have changed our lives and the lives of our family and friends. The messages have confirmed the validity of our own personal experiences. They ring true to us by the intuitive certainty which resonates deep within our core, speaking to eternal truth: we are not human beings having a spiritual experience—we are spiritual beings having a human experience.

Reginald H. Gray
Author

INTRODUCTION

The recorded messages you are receiving in this work are from spirits who once lived as humans on Earth and who have evolved to an elevation in high proximity with God. The messages explain our true origin and purpose on Earth. The goal of these spirits—which, thus, too, should be a goal of humankind—is to achieve a spiritual awakening—a critical mass of good.

"[Whilst] everything around me is ever changing, ever dying, there is underlying all that change a living power that is changeless, that holds all together, that creates, dissolves and recreates. That informing power or spirit is God....And is this power benevolent or malevolent? I see it as purely benevolent. For I can see that in the midst of death life persists, in the midst of untruth truth persists, in the midst of darkness light persists. Hence I gather that God is Life, Truth, Light. He is Love. He is the supreme Good."

— Mahatma Gandhi

1

GOD

Who and what is God? Is He the fear-inspiring judge of the Old Testament—the supreme arbiter of our lives—who made humans in His own image? Is He pure goodness and all-powerful? If so, why would he allow human suffering to exist or allow an innocent child to suffer pain or even die? Because of false ideas of the nature of the Divine, nonbelievers point to our miseries as proof that God cannot be the embodiment of goodness nor all-powerful. They conclude that the existence of earthly evils and human tragedy contradicts His very existence.

From the spirit messengers, we learn to think of God in a new ideal, one that is dissimilar from the Old Testament depiction of a vengeful, judgmental father sentencing us to hell for our transgressions.

With relief, we learn that God is a loving, creative, innocent source of pure perfection and energy who has always existed and who will continue forever. Best of all, we all have the Divine spark of God, our creator, in us.

But what of evil? Why does God allow it to cause suffering among His creations? It is this misunderstanding that the messengers first address in their communications with us. They are adamant to explain how a loving God does not conflict with the existence of evil.

The "God is good and yet humans suffer" dilemma was the basis for one of the first questions advanced to the messengers. The spirit messengers responded immediately in an unequivocal statement that at first seemed startling.

You are definitely wrong; emphatically wrong.

They proclaim that a loving God would never think of making any one of His children, even the worst, undergo pain and suffering or allow misfortunes to come their way.

We often receive waves representing the most fantastic views regarding the Great One. There is nothing which is not attributed to Him: wickedness, deceit, illness, sufferings, the wish of punishment. How it darkens everything when such waves reach us. That mankind should dare to believe and teach such things time after time shows us the strength of evil influence.

God is not cognizant of suffering:

If you love a person, could you allow that person to suffer? Do you wish to punish that person? You would shudder and say: how can you believe such a thing of me, when you know of my devotion for him? Yet to Him, Who is only light and love, you attribute—or at least allow it to be believed—that He knows of your sufferings. Can you imagine pure love watching slow suffering, slow dying of flesh? It is terrifying to see that mankind should believe in such a God, Who to our view would be worse than evil, as to allow the torture of earthly souls and not stop it, would be a hundredfold worse than evil. But here comes the point men are reluctant to believe and that is that God has no knowledge of earthly souls' wickedness and could not interfere with their free will.

The belief that God sends pain is false:

We understand your anxiety that many people will lose the comforting thought that God sends the pain under which they suffer for their betterment, but do you not feel at heart that possibly just that belief is the one which estranges man from God? The man who thinks will ultimately always revolt against a God who allows suffering. Evil wants you to believe that God gives you suffering and at the same time wishes you to believe that it cannot be a god of all good. We feel a certainty in illuminating the world of this truth. It will make Christ bigger ultimately and

> will also make mankind realise that their attitude towards their fellow man carries their own happiness.

Man is responsible for his misery:

> When man will realise that his free will makes him and not God respon-
> sible for his acts, then only will the light of the Great One begin its
> unhindered shine on mankind. No one dared to tell man that he is the
> sole controller of his soul. If he realises that, purity will spread its roots
> to every heart, but this will take long, very long. God is love, light and
> mercy without sin. Do not look for your ill-doings in His heart.

God never sends sorrow to anyone and is wholly unaware of what suffering means and how it is incurred. No thought of anything connected with evil could enter that perfection in love and innocence which is the nature of the Great One. The truth of the cause of our problems and suffering on Earth, as we will see throughout the messages, is human imperfection and frailty. In other words, because of free will many of us choose to suffer and blame an outside source for that suffering. This superiority complex—or God complex—comes from an unhealthy attachment to the ego, resulting in spiritual separation from our higher self and an over-inflated sense of our smaller, material self. Once we learn to take responsibility for our lives, yielding humbly to the Great One by accepting the fact that we are mere parts of a larger creation, the suffering can end.

God's Comprehension of Evil

Later, the messengers devote many statements to the reality of evil and evil's attempt to lead us away from the true path, which is God's. But is God aware of evil? The messengers state that God "knows no evil."

Fundamental to the messengers' definition of God is that He is the sole reality, which was, is, and will be indestructible; otherwise, He would not be God. What He holds or what emanates from Him is everlasting and is the only substance which cannot suffer decay and annihilation, but what does not belong to him in any respect is temporary and must, for that reason, be considered an illusion, and has nothing of the eternal. It has no place in the real existence where God is all that is.

Pain, suffering, strife, and evil in its many shapes lie outside the knowledge of the Great One; thus, such experiences are an illusion, like a passing

3

shadow soon to disappear into oblivion or like a nightmare soon forgotten in the light of day.

Being human, we are still subject to doubts that creep into the mind. We wonder whether God lacks omniscience and omnipotence if He is ignorant of evil and the very real sufferings of His creations.

The answer to this uncertainty comes promptly from the other side:

> God is omniscient and omnipotent only as far as goodness is concerned; evil does not come into question with Him. The human ideas of omnipotence and omniscience in every respect are not the truth. Mankind invented them, because to them it is not absolute love, but absolute power, which makes the greatest impression. It is that which they believe to be the key to the mastering of the world and the universe.

According to this statement, the omniscience of the Great One concerns reality; illusions do not exist as they are not reality. What is not everlasting reality is invisible to Him, a part of some darkness, which is not even perceived and cannot be apprehended. Evil is not intelligible to absolute purity and innocence.

Per the messengers, it is wrong of us to think that omniscience means knowledge of everything—bad as well as good. If God were anything but pure love, truth, and reality, this would be so.

Love is omnipotent in the world of eternity and is the one "power" outside the scope of temporary, perishable conditions. But omnipotence—a very misused term—can only operate according to the nature of the omnipotent Being. A God of pure innocence, who knows no evil, cannot fight it or He would not be pure innocence. Power is not love; therefore, is not an ultimate force. Haven't we seen that this is true on Earth? Mere power without love has never been in power for long. If such a force can keep order and peace for good, then "might is right;" but it never was, and as on Earth, so in the Universe and in the highest spheres. In the world of absolute reality, love keeps all moving and progressing in harmony without dictated laws. God's power comes from the love He gives and inspires.

How could evil be crushed by sheer power? It is of a spiritual nature and, like good, is present in the souls of men. Force does not bend our wills. Our individuality would revolt against it. Even the Great One cannot break the free will of a created being by the application of force, but His love may force all to unite in love. We must not in our world of illusions calculate as if the rules and conditions we lay down were also valid in a realm of reality which is not comparable to existence on Earth.

Punishment and Retribution

The view which is preached from most pulpits in the Western world and still held to be true among many religious people, is that God in Heaven is a supreme judge of human thoughts and actions and deals with man according to his merits, faults, and actions here on Earth. It is our instinctive sense that we must have something higher than ourselves which may be safely entrusted with the delicate task of sorting bad from good that accounts for this traditional view of God as judge.

We are told in the messages, which are clear on this point, that this belief is wrong, and the logic behind such an idea is false. The logic is faulty because, God, whose love draws us toward Him, cannot also be a judge who punishes. We are too quick in forming conclusions from our earthly experiences and taking as a pattern of the Divine order the model of institutions that we ourselves have set up.

The Great One only knows goodness and would not inflict punishment, the like one reads of in the Bible.

God cannot punish as He knows no sin.

Punishment is inflicted by your own self going from a different route from that in which and through which God shines.

God knows no evil, nor pain, nor misery. Man brought himself to suffering by hearkening to evil's temptation.

Although He is unaware of evil, He is aware of spirits shunning His light and it is for that He sent so much beauty down to Earth so that even there, where He is not truly wanted by the multitude, Divine beauty should remind them of what they shall receive if they believe in pure love and love for the sake of love.

They describe God as an entity of light and love. Knowing no evil, He is unable to punish that which He is unaware of.

In a lighter moment, the messengers speak almost in verse, describing a God of innocence:

> He is Light and All,
>
> He is Goodness,
>
> He is Art,
>
> He is Beauty,
>
> He is Melody,
>
> He is Poetry and
>
> He is one big Heart,
>
> He is most of all a Child.

This is a picture of God that we are not accustomed to imagining. What do they mean, "He is most of all a child"?

They want us to envision an innocence of such purity that it knows no innocence; a light of such potency that it is unaware of light; a knowledge of such magnitude that it ceases to be conscious knowledge; a power so strong that it has no sense of power; a love so selfless that it is nature; a perfection so perfect that it perfects itself.

The Divine cannot be aware of its own attributes, as nothing else exists in reality. God radiates light, love, and beauty with supreme innocence. Humility as well as tenderness are parts of His nature. His activity is innocent joy in creating, though He is unaware of even this in a human sense of the word.

As the messengers so eloquently state:

> Such perfection as God is can only exist if unaware of it. The instant you are aware of such things you have opponents and are not alone in your powers. The proof of His omniscience is that He knows not of it and His heavenly mathematics are equally without His knowledge. He creates without His knowledge, but this must not be interpreted in earthly words. The Great One is true knowledge just as He is pure love, but if He is true knowledge in the sense of the Divine, He cannot be aware of it, because if He were, it would not be truly divine. He is not aware of His knowledge nor of His power, hence His absolute

humbleness of which He is equally unaware. God is unaware that He is all and light and emanates light the same way.

The Great One combines everything which is beauty, light, goodness, and love. He is like a source not only for one attribute but He is all. It is for us to realise His divinity, His absolute love, knowledge, light.

The messengers at this point, as if they themselves are taken aback by their own knowledge, ask:

Is it possible for man to understand something so enormous as the Great One?

We are warned to avoid earthly conditions and comparisons when we contemplate the Divine:

Do not imagine that God sits up all-exclusive in His omnipotence awaiting His subjects to come and worship Him like kings on Earth. He is unaware of His absoluteness and only knows love and beauty and gathers them around and towards Him. That we [the spirits] all draw towards Him is a natural fact.

God is the origin of happiness and he who yearns for it shall live in bliss and lightness like a feather gaily flying in the air guided by the force of the wind.

God lays down no laws which would sound as a deliberate ruling power. The laws of God are the natural immersions of love and light.

"I live and love in God's peculiar light."

— Michelangelo

2

LIGHT

The concepts of light and love are recurring themes throughout the messages. God as light and love is touched upon briefly at this point. Later, when describing their own "lives," the spirits elaborate on the role of light in the spirit world.

For example, a message says:

> Imagine a colossal Globe of fire and love which draws to Itself what is in harmony with It. That Globe of love and light knows no forcing, no violence. It calls for love and light and the rest lies with us.

This is the nearest symbolic impression which the communicating spirits may bring us about God, but it would be incorrect, we are told, to take this paragraph in a literal sense. The messengers tell us that we should try to grasp their verbalization of God and their attempt to describe him in earthly terms by our imagination and intuitive inner sense, not with literal intellectual analysis. This same qualification applies to every one of the qualities of God. We are to try to place our intellect aside and seek an understanding through our inner awareness—through our most primal instincts of soul consciousness imbued in ourselves as divine beings.

When we can grasp that the fundamental attributes of God are light and love, we approach what the messengers mean by light in this respect and by love of a divine quality in contrast to the common definition of love.

God's essence of being light and love is a statement confirmed by Christ and other great spiritual teachers of the past.

Modern science describes the nature of matter as particles at their most fundamental level existing as waves or quanta of energy. The intensity of the vibrations of the waves determines whether or not we can observe the particles as "solid" matter or measurable energy.

Whether the Divine light consists of waves and particles, we do not know for sure, but it would appear that the infinite energy and vibrations of God create ultimate Light, which inexorably filters through the universe. This Divine emanation is perceived not only by the spirits but by humans on Earth. We embrace God's Light on both a sensory level and more subtly in our souls when we experience love, happiness, joy, optimism, enthusiasm, awe, reverence, charity, and the many finer, noble emotions which humans can create for themselves and their loved ones. The messengers consider these uplifting states of mind gifts from God, endowed by the free will imparted to each human when the Divine spark imbued our biological forms with an eternal soul.

The spirit messengers often refer to "waves," "shooting rays," and "vibrations" when describing God's emanations and the spirits' perception of both earthly and cosmic exchanges.

Along these lines, the messengers say:

> God manages all the stars through His light and gives light to the sun. The great inspirations are the light of God becoming visible.

> The light of God is ever moving and it shoots out continual waves in circle formation. The circle is the symbol of eternity without a beginning and without an end. How many are pure enough to catch one glimpse of that circular light?

> When our thoughts are filled with love and we forget ourselves it may happen that we meet directly with the light of the Great One and only that can give a happiness which is disconnected from Earth.

The messengers continue to try to explain Divine light. In a beautiful conclusion, they tell of the Divine affinity and connection we have with God:

He creates through His light and love, and all the glorious emotions which run through you are emanating from Him.

Another way to describe elemental nature is that it consists of vibrations or rays, as the messengers do in their descriptions of spirit bodies and means of communication, God's essence, the heavenly spheres, and the fabric of the soul. All that we consider solid and material, including our bodies is energy, expressed by the vibrations of waves of varying intensity or frequency. Therefore, by acting from a place of love while on Earth, we can move our vibrations closer to that of the Divine Light.

"Love is composed of a single soul inhabiting two bodies."

— Aristotle

3

LOVE

If it were possible to draw a line between Divine love and human love and define the way in which human affections differ from God's love, we could better realize the nature of God. However, the messengers inform us that love between humans on Earth is not the love of God, which is absolute. They distinguish Divine and selfless love from the model of love that some of us mistakenly hold to be "true" love, while it appears that it is, for lack of a better term, "false" love; a love which is absorbing and has sad limitations.

Human love has different qualities and stages but the moment it is mingled with the slightest ill-feeling, it is no longer the pure love that the messengers regularly speak of. Many of us on Earth have the love from God within, yet, we entertain the voice of evil, and therefore, earthy love cannot be absolute, though it can be great.

"The voluntary servants of God," as they call themselves, "Who is love and light," are better judges than we and their comments on the topic are illuminative and concise:

> Love rules and love that comes from the light of the Great One knows no ambition, envy or jealousy, but wishes to give and serve without limitations, an unselfish and charitable love.

> Love combines every quality that belongs to the highest spheres.

From love have all good things been given birth. From love came beauty, humbleness, charity, and all the arts.

Love is something that can be concrete, that can be liquid, can be visible and invisible, touched and untouchable at the same time. Love is eternal light which burns its light in darkness just as in daylight. Only love without fear, jealousy, envy, and self-obsession continue to be love in this world.

Real love has no wish to rule over others.

Pure love is self-giving. It is tolerant and forgets its ego and consequently it shoots and radiates happiness around and with it. That is the love which evil shuns and cannot touch.

Selflessness is true Godliness. Sacrifice is love. Real love is real tact. Love must always be spontaneous and unexpected.

Love is never at a standstill. It shoots its waves in billions of variations. It is ardent, burning, gentle, enveloping wholly and partly, yet seen in such strength it is often mixed with other attributes, and so it raises higher one moment and sinks the next, and your knowledge improves and falls back accordingly.

True love is from the spirit, and the spirit never tires.

There is only one God from Whom all love and light emanates, Who is wisdom and innocence. Accept that and refrain from analysing as that will not make you better, but will occupy your time, which you can use more valuably. You get warmth from the sun and you gladly accept it, but you cannot become a sun yourself, no matter how much you analyse, and if you are too sure of yourself and insist in looking on it too long, you will be blinded.

The messengers go on to explain that if we cultivate a love that gives, we shoot out vibrating waves charged with this "giving love," regardless of our own desires—though including them—and this spreads a light in all directions, which we cannot see but which is doing invaluable benefit to mankind. This love naturally conquers every other kind because it is not limited to one path or one subject but emanates from all sides and angles. This is the love that has the most resemblance to the love of God.

Giving love allows the freedom of the waves from every pore of your body within and without, whilst the absorbing love sucks through the brain everything it can for its own benefit and instead of light around there is darkness.

Love is constant, calm, and brings light; whereas, evil is fickle: it is unsteady and in its restlessness, casts a mist of shadows around it, so as to mask its movements.

Where true love acts, evil becomes stunned and his waves scatter about and buds of beauty create rays shooting out into the universe.

Only through love can we arrive at truth and the understanding of God. Love leads the spirits to God. Mind is affected by ambitions, always trying to surpass others. It has no time for love.

If we have no love to give, we cannot be happy.

Love can be acquired by telling gradually those who care only for material possessions that God dwells in all of us. Only through modesty and meekness and unselfish love can mankind approach the light of God. Those who can love on Earth allow the Divine to shine in them.

If you are good, you have love in you; and if you have love in you, you have God in you, and if you have God in you, you believe in Him.

The true religion of God is love.

"I am not this hair, I am not this skin, I am the soul that lives within."

— Rumi

4

CONSCIOUSNESS AND HARMONY OF THE SOUL AND BODY

The messengers offer that our individuality and consciousness is our soul. They describe the soul as being headquartered in our nervous system—specifically the brain—serving as the channel in which the light of our spirit can move within the body. The brain, as an instrument for registering and displaying our soul, was so meticulously fashioned according to heavenly mathematics, that our soul remains simultaneously connected to our body and to the Divine.

We learn that the power of the soul is isolated from the energy needed by the physical body to perform its functions. Thus, when the physical body expires, the soul is freed with its consciousness and individuality unimpaired from the changes within the mortal form. The soul possesses, as a heritage from God, a mind and memory, constituting a continuity of experience which is eternal. Simply stated, the personality of the individual survives death and manifests itself in the spirit's essence.

> *It is this Consciousness of self, this Mind and Memory, which you characterize as personality, which grows and is molded into greater comprehension and power through the various cycles of evolution. Each incarnation, spirit to mortal to spirit, enables the soul to advance and strengthen its moral, divine goodness. Eventually, as was achieved*

17

by Jesus Christ, man's evil tendencies are completely cleansed through these mortal sojourns on Earth by the ever-increasing judicious employment of the free will.

Can individuality be attributed to God who made us individuals?

Your question we will try to answer, but do not imagine that we know everything. We have endless studies before we can grasp God, but we can tell you what we have already learnt. That the Great One combines everything which is beauty, light and goodness, and love—we have told you before. He is to our view like a Source but a source not only in one— or rather for one—attribute. He is all. Now if you receive the free will from Him, which—more or less—gives you individuality and makes you individual, He must be and is the Source of individuality Himself. Everything, except what is evil, comes and is continually coming out of Him. He gives unceasingly.

Individuality is in one respect the nearest image of the Great One, and on Earth no one possesses that attribute to the likeness of the high spirits.

You seem surprised at the idea of angels, spirits who never were on Earth, being highly individual. You think that because you serve God, the Great One, you either love individuality or never possessed it. Why do you think such a theory? You can live and work in perfect harmony though you are individual and not equal in goodness, light, etc. As long as evil is absent, individuality can be mixed and benefit by mixing and give continual varieties. If you work for the same purpose, individuality helps greatly. You on Earth, who work mostly through mechanism, cannot grasp this statement. The Great One is so far beyond anything you can imagine that His light can feed for eternity the variety of individuals and individuality. It is the part of Him in them that makes individuality and augments His light.

Into the physical body comes the Soul with its Personality, its perfect memory of all past experiences and its acquired penalties and rewards earned through the law of compensation.

The law of compensation is a natural law which requires a balancing of evil earthly deeds with amends and moral restitution while in mortal form, which you are allowed to accomplish using your God-given free will. As long as an incarnated soul endeavors to balance and off-set evil done in prior incarnations, the soul is gradually elevated and eventually that soul has earned residence in the highest spheres and is relieved of further earthly lives. Jesus Christ was the highest evolved soul ever to return to mortal existence, which He chose to do to experience mortal suffering in the belief and hope that His example would hasten the spiritual evolution of mankind.

It is evident that Christ descended to Earth with His heavenly Personality, Mind and Memory intact, fully cognizant of His intimate proximity to God and the blessed realm. He came to Earth on His own free will. While His mission was premature, His life has inspired mankind in a profound and lasting legacy which man would be advised to emulate.

We must grasp the fact that other qualities than those we are endowed with belong to the Supreme, for He gives light and life from which everything is created in a never-ending flow which had no beginning.

How can we have a part of God within us, yet understand God's individuality which seems to separate us from Him? Perhaps the following analogy will help explain this apparent dichotomy.

Imagine the ocean on a cloudless day. The sun's disk is mirrored on the glassy veneer. Then a slight breeze ruffles the surface, and the water is gently rippled. The single image of the sun is suddenly replaced by a sea of miniature suns, each perfectly reproduced on the undulations. All are reflections of a single source—a part of the blazing life-giving star whose sphere Earth orbits.

Like our sun, God's individual light is reflected in the ocean of humanity. Our souls are a microcosmic manifestation of His light, the source of our life. The spirits will shortly describe humans' divinity as a spark of God. Imbued with His gift of life we are as individual as a sparkling wavelet while also a part of the entire ocean, each of us reflecting the spark of God.

God is the great dynamic force, constantly on the move, advancing and progressing in itself. He draws life toward a perpetual advance in individual qualities. There is no status quo about the Great One within the mansions of Heaven. Activity increases the higher we rise seeking to be near His sphere. Few—if any—spirits reach His level, because even as our souls individually evolve and advance toward His light, God Himself is also continually elevating His perfection.

God is individual, but cannot be aware of His individuality in the same way that we are because nothing exists outside Him in the world of reality. Nothing but God exists in that realm: He is the One, the ultimate sum of all individualities, individual Himself, although without limitations.

The messengers explain that what makes the body function is the spirit, which, naturally, the physical eye cannot see, but which without the flesh possesses infinitely stronger everything of value, that is love and beauty in the true sense, music, passion, etc. All these are independent of the body.

> As on Earth you enter flesh, they use flesh—or rather the organs—as medium. None of you feel love, enjoy music, poetry, etc., with the body, but having a body so gloriously calculated for enabling the spirit to demonstrate all heavenly sensations, it becomes impossible for souls to understand that in reality the flesh is the barrier for complete advance. The spirit never sleeps.

> We heard your talks about the work of the brain and your friend's comment regarding it. Her belief almost gives an importance to the organs as if they would follow you to spirit-life. The organs of the body are nothing more or less than the instrument through which the multitude of waves find free route for entering and going out. The brain works on the same system, but what goes through it is the most vital part of the ego, as it represents your spirit which demonstrates its value by the strength and length of the circular waves. This is why you can remember things, as all which enters or leaves the channels, called brain, is your spirit. Nothing of that is ever lost as it is yourself. It does not take, or rather it does not need, space as it is space.

> Feelings which you all have are following you for eternity. If it were the nerves, who are giving you feelings, once you had a feeling and it is past, you could not have a recurrence of the same feeling. The nerves are there to serve as an instrument for the feelings of your soul to pass through your whole body. It is so minutely calculated in such heavenly mathematics that brain, nerve, muscle can react simultaneously to the waves of the soul.

The nerves are the only channel that light (which is your soul) can pass. That is why sensations and impressions are so variable. If your sensations would be the functions of your nerves, the nerves being practically the same in all humans, could that then vary so greatly?

The brain is the receptive instrument for registering or displaying your soul or spirit. Therefore, we say that the thoughts are more important than what you actually disclose to your fellow-man. It is waves that keep your body attached to your spirit and only if these waves are pure and in harmony can your brain act the same.

The brain is the mechanical receiver for the humans, but has not to do with thought or memory. The brain has been created for the registering of happenings on Earth. That which vibrates your whole being, that urges you to better yourself and most of all the love which raises all to higher regions, could never act through the brain. When the brain perishes, constructive thoughts are retained and through the power of waves ever circulating in the ether we can pick up memories of the past.

Your conscience works through your brain whilst we vibrate our waves all around you and right inside you. We never use your brain as a medium. The instant you begin to analyse, our waves get disturbed by your doubts.

You agree that very few know and believe that any voices they hear within themselves are the direct waves of influence from the world of the soul's awakening and though perfectly conscious of those feelings, voices, or you may call it whatever you like, they attribute it to the subconscious and believe that they are themselves influencing their lives and actions. You see the absurdity of a conscious subconscious.

Nevertheless, it stands valid and even some of the cleverest scientists vouch for the validity of such a statement, and why? Simply because by stating such doctrines they get out of a difficulty they cannot solve.

Difficulty, yes for those who reject and are bored with the simple truth and want to ornate that which becomes thus distorted and a riddle to most people.

There are, so to speak, two personalities in each soul. You would call that the conscious and the subconscious, which, however, is not the case.

They both are conscious but one is occupied with earthly things, material work in time; the other, though you know it works and thus it is not subconscious, works outside time, as it has the speed that no time can register, and you pay little attention to it, yet it is the building up of the ...no better said ...is the progress of your spirit which, though attached to the body, does its work independently.

Let us talk about the energy condensed in every soul. To start with if that energy would be used you could not remain on Earth, as your physical body is not capable of using all the energy stored up in you. Are you aware that in each of you everything you achieve, when a spirit, is stored up, or better said, locked up in you—are in this respect even with you? Past and future are non-existing and that is the reason why you get occasionally the impression that certain events have been lived through before by you. One cannot let that energy completely free as it belongs to the spiritual existence and one's body on Earth would be incapable of doing its work if this energy, being from the spirit, would be let free, but it does not mean that one must shut up all doors for its outlet and a gradual disciplined opening to use that energy is not prohibited and the time—as you say on Earth—has arrived to study closely these powers of energy and to use them in much greater force than hitherto.

Many scientists declare that such images pertain to the subconscious, not realising that what they call subconscious must gather from somewhere what it reveals. That material cannot be born from nothing as such does not exist. The energy which we talk of lives with us, but it is stored up in you.

Remember your flesh perishes, but the waves are always there and can freely learn with us, as they do not depend on time or space or anything material. Your energy is the receiver of our talks. Up here, these talks are shared by all, but on Earth they can only reach you by the use of the stored-up energy.

"Far superior to the pleasures and rewards of the illusion that is earthly life, are the pleasure and rewards of the Reality."

— Ian Gardner

5

THE WORLD OF REALITY

God cannot be identified with anything perishable. The messengers have described reality as only that which exists within the sphere of the Great One. All else is temporary and, thus, an illusion. It follows then that the present universe, being perishable, is an illusion. He would exist had there been no Big Bang and will remain when the physical universe vanishes, as physicists say will eventually happen—according to the second law of thermodynamics, e.g., entropy. He is, spiritually speaking, outside it all and independent of the so-called material world. A spiritual realm is in perpetual being beyond the material. It is imperishable; it is Reality.

In this chapter, the messengers describe with captivating clarity the world of God as they understand Him. Was there a beginning, and if so, how did it happen? Why was individual life called into being; are we or God responsible for our fate? What is the nature of the transcendent world? What is death and is it final? Does immortality include pre-existence?

Those who speak to us from beyond the veil have pondered these questions just as we do. The issues were important when they too, were flesh. But now we have the sublime good fortune to learn by the spirits' experience and are told what is known in the high spheres. Despite their sometimes clear frustration with the Earth-bound appreciation of things spiritual, they patiently detail their revelations.

This they do, we are informed, because the precarious situation on Earth compels us to acquire a clear vision of reality so that we can hasten the development of our spiritual comprehension.

Does the physical universe have a separate existence or is it a part of God?

> *Is the Great One outside it? Yes, in one respect and no in another. The Great One is both in and outside the Universe. He is outside where evil dominates but within where goodness dwells.*
>
> *Now, in a brief resume you will find that we are justified in declaring that the Great One is both connected and disconnected from Earth. We told you that only the perishable is an illusion. Everything else is emanating from the Great One, but do not forget that the Great One has innumerable Messengers working, and progress is constant, though there never was a beginning.*
>
> *The Great One is outside it all [the universe], yet embraces the whole because He is the circle and from whatever view you try to look at things, He is always there. You know the saying: 'The eyes of God are everywhere'—a very common remark, but true and originates from reminiscences when you were a spirit.*

Is the circle what the spirit world may conceive of God and everything existing inside the orbit of that circle?

> *You ask about the circle. Of course the Great One is outside it all and the drawing into His circle cannot be put into language.*
>
> *Energy is the domain of God and is the divine source. Everything is drawn out of it and everything is supported by it.*
>
> *Enthusiasm is coming from the divine source and if you dwell on it, you approach the circle of the Great One. Has not God created the spirits from a perpetual enthusiasm? Were He to slacken—which is of course impossible—it would not be divine.*
>
> *Everything, even the Great One, is progressing. He in Himself and others through events, experiences and mostly from His light.*
>
> *The Great One is perfecting His perfection.*

26

Now you know that God is all power and so it is but power in love, goodness, light and continual progress. The picture we have of God is: advance and progress.

Love is omnipotent because it means progress.

God works unceasingly.

The Great One is alone, but all things come from Him.

The whole being of God is receiving as He conceives. That act is perpetual with Him in the most beautiful sense of the word.

When we arrive here, what strikes us most is that the higher you are, the less you know of it, just as God is unaware of His absoluteness. It does not lessen our worship for Him. There is no superiority and that One big Whole which we all feel and receive light from is unaware of superiority. This must be clear to you.

Is there a divine purpose to our lives and a design that has been established by God?

The Great One, Who is in continual motion, created and creates continually, spirits to collaborate with Him and from Him. You say: Why did He wish to create spirits at all? But that is a very weak and thoughtless question. Do you not—even on Earth—when you are loving something in the true sense wish to keep or multiply that which you love and do you not wish to share with many that which you love? So the Great One gives birth to spirits from the love He is and from the progress He is and for sharing what He is. The Great One knows that you all must follow Him as you are part of Him and that which lives with you on Earth and becomes once more the spirit after leaving Earth is just a spark of His own light but possessed with such strength that it can never be extinguished.

The Great One is experimenting unceasingly and will do so for eternity, moving in a circle without a beginning and without an end but at the same time expanding that circle. He is perfecting His own perfection and here man enters to develop that perfection into more perfection.

God creates because love must create and share all good things.

27

Picture to yourself all this greatness of God and feel that from it there is a continual emanation of sparks, each becoming a spirit. That is why we declare that everyone has a spark of God in him. The spark becomes a spirit with the free will accompanying it and in a microscopic way you possess the quality of the Great One with the exception that you cannot give life or light.

Is the quality of each spark from which a spirit develops originally decided by God?

Your present question is the very one we expected you to put. Here is the moment of realising the absolute absence of anything mechanical emanating from the Great One. No two sparks of the Great One, except very rarely, are alike and, therefore, no spirits resemble each other. The development of the spirits is left to the free will, and if you follow His light from the start, you advance rapidly and dwell high up. If you reject His light, you follow evil and as a natural cause descend to Earth or go elsewhere. The sparks vary in strength, in swiftness, and in magnitude, so naturally does the spirit, born from the spark.

Is the spark and the spirit in reality the same thing?

Same thing. Do not embrace everything so literally. No spark has anything but beauty in it. Its development has the rest of the work and the fight with evil and its temptations.

Are the sparks the living thoughts of the Great One?

No, how could they be thoughts? Thought is for Earth and not celestial. We do not know exactly ourselves how and what each spark represents and learn about it as we progress, not, however, through curiosity, but because the conditions or rather the work of the spirits tends towards illumination. What seems to us as the best explanation for man on Earth is that each spark is the breath of God, yet this is but a poor comparison as breathing belongs to Earth and is not needed up here.

Shall we rather say that each spark is part of the Great One's never-ceasing vibrations? But whatever we say is really not corresponding with the truth of it all, which cannot be compared.

That free will has been given to spirits to our view only strengthens the absolute good, purity, selflessness and love of God, because He gives through such a gift the freedom to advance and the development of each spirit to be individual. Each of you could become little individual gods as you are part of God, just as He is part of you.

The actual creation can only be done by the Great One and as He is creating, because it is part of His essence, it cannot be explained or else, were it known, it would have a beginning and an end. If that were so, God would be temporary and if He is temporary, He is not God. Grasp this in the most simple manner and you will be freed from a mystery man created himself.

God creates because He always was, as we told you before. We are satisfied to believe that it never started, as eternity can only be without a start or else it is not eternity, so if one leaves flesh behind and reaches the world of spirits, one grasps this statement without an effort.

Eternity is truth, hence it cannot be discussed but must be accepted. The instant you can discuss it, it ceases to be eternal and the complete truth. Naturally for those living on Earth, surrounded by perishables, prevented by opposite waves to advance, progress, etc. without discussions and controversies, it becomes practically impossible to accept a fact which is so true that it cannot be discussed. But this is the beauty we find here and which to those, who fully trust, on arrival up here opens immediately the road of eternal progress, hence following Him, Who always was and shall be and Whose innocence is not fermented by minds of evil followers.

We are not aware of being part of God before we became conscious.

We told you that creation always happened and that it must be thus accepted. The second point is: has—or rather—is the Great One responsible for any of us? First of all, you are part of God and so as God always was and always will be, cannot be accused of what He is, as you are part of that eternity.

The word 'creation' loses its meaning if nothing happens in the act of creation.

The messengers warn that there is much that will seem contradictory in their details concerning creation but they attempt to inform us further.

The Great One is creation and everything out of that creation is created, though it always was and will be. Now that you have a stronger idea of the Great One perhaps you will find it easier to grasp the meaning of the word 'creation'. It is used more for earthly purpose than for spiritual existence because up here one knows and realises the oneness with God and that there is no purpose of being created, but the cause is that the eternal produces eternally, and as He is that force, which is the essence of force, produces other forces which—if in contact with the main force—become again or continue to be part of it.

Now, we stated previously that each spirit is a spark of God, hence we say each spark creates a spirit, but that spark always was and always will be, so that if we reflect, we understand clearer that, though we seem to come away with the spark from God, we, through that magnetic bond we call the heavenly circle, are still the same as before the spark left and it is that which eventually returns, yet is absolutely individual.

Was it not individual as a spark?

God, we, through that magnetic bond we call the heavenly circle, are still the same as before the spark left and it is that which eventually returns, yet is absolutely individual.

Oh, yes. That is what you on Earth can never and will never understand and therefore just accept it. You still imagine God something small. We do not mean quite the earthly conception of small, yet small enough to compare things with the great doings of great souls on Earth. There you make your mistake. We cannot grasp the vastness of the Great One and the truth that He embraces the universe and that His circle combines all. What is outside this circle is the field of evil, which, as it is ultimately consumed, because it is perishable, we call it an illusion. We told you that by and by we shall tell you more and more difficult facts, so you must think about our statements and draw your own conclusions.

We now see that creation had no beginning and it will never end, as it is the nature of God to create—to create for the sake of love, progress, and increased perfection. It is an eternal activity outside time and knowledge which the spirits describe. As a part of God, we may participate in this continual process, which they call creation, although they are uncomfortable using an earthly term for a celestial concept.

The Great One is the essence of all that lives eternally. We are imbued with this essence, explaining our persistent search for meaning, for something greater than ourselves as we struggle with our corporeal, grounded existence on this planet. We seek contact with the spirit world and with God because of our common connection with Him, however indiscernible this Divine affiliation may seem at times.

We emerge from a Divine spark of His light, an integral part of Him, a spark that has always been and can never be extinguished. We are therefore not only immortal from an earthly perspective, but always existing as individuals while of the Great One.

The spirits define creation to the development of sparks, or souls, from conscious, but not self-conscious activity in the light of God, giving us a life controlled by free will, granted for our self-directed advancement and self-willed participation in the creative process.

It therefore appears that creation is a feature of God's constant drive towards perfection, or perfecting perfection, as the spirits put it. Creation is an incessant, natural unfolding of the Divine in which we, as separate beings, have been called forth to share freely in a universal progress. By our own individual development, we increase the light and perfection of God, staying a part of Him, though bestowed with an unalterable free will.

Unfortunately, as we know from experience here on Earth, free will is a gift that can be misused and involves great risk in its handling. It opens possibilities to drift away from His light, annulling the intentions of God.

On the other hand, it should be clear to us that this gift, this invitation from the Source to cooperate in the progressive perfection of purity, was certainly destined to enable us to accelerate the general advance of all things good. Free will instills in us the opportunity to develop the facility to love, and as the spirits make clear, love only breathes and truly grows in an environment of absolute freedom and self-conscious devotion. Free will is essential to our individuality and nourishes the advancement of variety in our enterprises, powers our inventive energy and supports our endeavors to enhance our lives.

Know that all that emanates from the essence of God is everlasting and must ultimately, however far it travels, return to His magnetic light. The Great One could not have doubted the inevitable result of His gift

of parts of Himself to us. Inspired by the certainty of increasing perfection by this act, He made the experiment, an act outside knowledge
and time.

Our spark of divinity, becoming our soul, compels us to recognize that
our own fate rests within ourselves. We are fractions of the Divine
exercising free will within its limits. We cannot blame the Great One
and pass off responsibility for the pain our actions cause. He dwells in
us and acts in keeping with the perfection of His nature. Being an actual part of Him in a true spiritual sense, admonishing Him for our
pains and sorrows is meaningless. Whatever tribulations we meet
on our path are not sent by God. They are caused by a misuse of
our free will.

The messengers repeatedly emphasize this truth—that we ourselves are
the masters of our fate, rising if we develop the individual evolution of
our souls towards good, and sinking if we are swayed by the temptations of evil and away from God's light; descending until we find the
will to change; to choose the path of eternal progress.

"If Christ Jesus dwells in a man as his friend and noble leader, that man can endure all things, for Christ helps and strengthens us and never abandons us. He is a true friend."

— St. Teresa of Avila

6

JESUS CHRIST'S TRUE NATURE

Next we are to learn about the true nature of Christ, who He was, why He came down to Earth, what He was trying to accomplish and the nature of the supreme sacrifice He made to enlighten our lives to our true heritage.

We have learned in the messages that God is not aware of the illusion of mortal life because material things are temporary and thus do not exist in the realm of Divine reality. Even in the highest spheres, near the Great One, very little of our experiences on Earth is known, for pain and suffering, all the attributes of evil, are entirely ignored. Nor would a spirit near the lofty heights of God consider soiling the purity of the Divine abode by reports of the state of events on Earth and other low places. The Source of innocence, love and light, on which all depends, cannot be approached with tales from our world of illusion and evil. Near God such things could never be grasped. When you think about it, even we find quite unbelievable the depravity, brutality and atrocity man is capable of inflicting on fellow humans. How often have we watched the evening news with revulsion and changed the channel to insulate ourselves from the horror? Is it so difficult then to understand the high spirits protecting the celestial realm from evil narrative? This does not mean that the spirits are unaware of earthly events. Our messengers and their purpose in these exchanges are evidence of that fact. Thus, Jesus knew of earthly suffering, and even though He dwells closest to the light of God, being the most evolved of God's creations, He hurt for us and our travails and ignorance of our true nature.

His concern and love for humankind became the wonderful, self-sacrificing act that has endeared us to Him for 2,000 years. Jesus was free to still be near God for eternity, having fulfilled his karmic balancing required by God's law of compensation. Instead, He undertook His mission to Earth, wanting to inform and educate man of the true nature of the world of reality and show through His life and death the length to which a love goes which emanates from the Source of love and light. He was especially intent on making man understand that a Heavenly Father is eternally waiting to embrace them in His ceaseless love and care, enlisting them to join Him in the progress toward a perfection which brings happiness in itself.

Though there have been others who descended for the benefit of humanity, Christ has captured our admiration and reverence and becomes for many of us the truest and most worshipful example of Divine character and the heavenly covenant.

What we know of Jesus, however, is the result of translations of translations of oral stories which became the books of the New Testament, some written four hundred years after His death. It is not necessarily an exact account of Jesus' life and teachings. Religions which grew from His influence have further altered some of His teachings' meaning and drawn conclusions that benefit their dogma at the expense of truth.

As we learned earlier, God dwells in all of us, the soul being a spark from His expanding light and that we are, in a sense, parts of the Great One. Thus, God is still the true Father of each individual soul and spirit, the highest as well as the lowest. Christ, knowing better than anyone else that God was His Father, came particularly to us to bring knowledge of this Truth. But Christ, though the nearest to God and the only one who is said to have "seen God," was not the Ultimate Being Himself in the meaning of the Holy Trinity.

We may now learn much of the meaning of the life of Jesus and his spiritual nature in the words of the messengers.

> *God was the Father of Christ, but not in the sense you believe. We are all sons and daughters of Him, though when you arrive to purification*

man and woman become one, but the Great One is in them. Christ wanted us to understand that, but men made a complicated story of the real truth. Christ was and is the nearest to the Great One and His incomparable love for spirits and souls on Earth was so great that He wished to make the supreme sacrifice.

The only spirit Who was in direct contact with God was Christ. Christ was the one and only Who from birth was perfectly free from any malice, any envy or personal ambition, and wholly enveloped in love of the divine sort, finding comfort in helping mankind. He was the interpreter of God, but religion as it stands is completely ignorant of the truth. No man before or since had the tolerance that Christ had and that was because He followed His Father and the Father of you all in that respect.

Christ was able to listen to His inner voice, which He knew was the direct voice of God. The same happened to Buddha. That their teachings are somewhat alike is not to be wondered at considering that both listened to the same voice. They each had their own imagination, suiting the people of their time.

When Christ descended to Earth He became man, but the recollection of His existence as the nearest messenger to God never left Him and therefore one could never compare Him with any ordinary human. He entered the body of a truly loving and pure woman. It is true that that woman had the vision of an angel appearing to her and preparing her for the coming of the nearest messenger of God. The vision of Mary was in the shape of a dream. Christ knew exactly how His life on Earth would fare. He had to suffer for mankind as they were not ready to receive Him and so evil was victorious. When Christ exclaimed: 'Why hast Thou forsaken me?' it was because He felt pain for the first time and in His agony He had forgotten that the Father of all knows no pain. When His body got too weak to be controlled by the spirit then the nerves, being exposed to pain, made Him exclaim thus. His agony was of a very short duration as God received Him in His circle immediately.

No spirit would dare to approach that which is purity itself, only Christ can do that. The light of God cannot be looked at, except by Jesus Christ.

That Christ was actually God descending to Earth is a mistake and does not fit with (Swedenborg's) [1] *idea of God being one and not three in one.*

He obviously like many others misunderstood Christ's saying as to that part and elaborated it according to his own idea. If Christ was God, why would He have cried out at the last on the cross: 'Father why hast Thou forsaken me?' God cannot cry out to Himself: 'Father'.

First of all He is alone and has no father or mother. That belongs to flesh for earthly progeneration. Why does man on Earth insist in making God after their image? What conceit and what smallness of mind! Secondly, God knows no pain, no sufferings. How could Christ then be God? It is just there where you will find that Christ, though nearest to God, is not God Himself and that He in His agony of suffering forgot that God knew not that He was in pain. Is it not perhaps even more convincing how great a spirit Christ was. He who lived and shone in the brightest light would come down to set an example to mankind and give them the illumination for what is good and noble. Does not that prove to you more what those, who are filled with God, can do to redeem humanity?

That Christ is the Son of God, we have repeatedly told you, but we wish to make it clear that He is not more so than all souls on Earth. God does not know of favouritism. He gives the same to all. He could not be God would He not do so, because to have favourites, you must be acquainted with lesser good. Christ is in our eyes superior, because He like His Father is absolute love.

---

[1] **Swedenborg, Emanuel** (1688-1772), Swedish scientist, philosopher, and theologian, founder of the Swedenborgian sect. A man of unusual intellectual powers, Swedenborg made important contributions to mathematics, chemistry, physics, and biology. His Philosophical and Mineral Works (3 vol., 1734) contain his views on the derivation of matter. His studies in physiology led him to attempt, in Economy of the Animal Kingdom (2 vol., 1741), an explanation of the relationship between matter and the soul. In 1745, after claiming to have experienced supernatural visions, Swedenborg began to study theology. In Heavenly Arcana (8 vol., 1749-56), he propounded a religious system based on an allegorical interpretation of the Scriptures according to instructions professedly received from God. Swedenborg maintained that in 1757 the last judgment occurred in his presence, that the Christian church as a spiritual entity came to an end, and that a new church, foretold as the New Jerusalem in the Book of Revelation, was created by divine dispensation. According to Swedenborg, the natural world derives its reality from the existence of God, whose divinity became human in Jesus Christ. The highest purpose is to achieve conjunction with God through love and wisdom. Swedenborg died in London on March 29, 1772.

Jesus knew not of evil before coming to Earth and had no discussion with the Great One in the sense you imagine. But He was too swift in His acts and descended too early and therefore He had to suffer, as—once you descend—you cannot avoid suffering. Yes, He did come to see the world of sinners, though He himself knew not of sin.

He has now joined the Circle of God and He is one with the Great One but His waves of influence will go on and on in the universe as long as it is needed. This is what is difficult for you to grasp.

The Atonement

We know by now that God is not the severe sovereign on high who critically watches the ill acts of man and metes out the amount of punishment due to each per some Heavenly code of conduct. We are told earlier that God is the essence of innocence, love and light, and being unaware of evil is not thinking of punishment nor demanding to be appeased. He needs no sacrificial offerings for trespassing divine law.

How then, do we square this knowledge with the ancient doctrine of atonement? The belief that God sent his nearest to undergo suffering to deliver man from punishment for his own sins is simply wrong. How could the Great One, whose nature is so different from man's assumptions, have allowed Christ's suffering to undo the gift of free will? How could He "save" us from an evil He does not know exists? The concept of the atonement is contrary to the law of compensation and our own sense of justice. It was invented by man and has no foundation whatsoever in the nature of God. Atonement sprung from the fear of vindictive gods and should be abolished so that the real purpose of Christ's mission to Earth can be seen and appreciated in its true radiance.

Christ's message was one of love, that God is love and that nothing else is required of us but to accept this truth and absorb that love. When we do this, we adopt an attitude of life that brings harmony with the Source of our souls. There is no other way to achieve redemption. Not even Christ can shoulder the responsibility of another individual or undergo the punishment which naturally follows in the wake of sins.

The messengers make it very clear that we are responsible for ourselves. Vicarious atonement is of no value to the individual character. We must strengthen our will and elevate our attitude, by drastic measures, if necessary. Only by self-directed effort to improve and advance can we traverse the path of lasting and continuous progress towards God.

Our individual nature is not altered by the intervention of another. Only by an act of will can we affect our nature, though we may certainly be influenced by the example of others. Christ was the ultimate example. He has offered compelling inspiration which has changed many human lives.

His arrival from the highest sphere, oblivious to everything but love and light, to an evil- plagued place to be crucified by the hands of ungrateful, ignorant humans was a unique and supreme sacrifice, unparalleled in all eternity. He proved what divine love means and His loss resounded down the centuries, opening man's eyes to the road we must enter to become reconciled with a God of love. A God Who needs nothing more but a wish from man to harmonize with His nature. If this desire is genuine, the possibilities open at once to loving help from the Great One.

It appears from the messages that Christ's mission was bound to fail as to the response he expected from the humans on Earth at that time. The wisdom of God knew the results of Christ's premature journey, but love of a divine nature cannot be forestalled and Christ surrendered to His intense desire to help souls on Earth, even though He was warned of the consequences.

Here now are the messages on this theme:

> *Christ came down against His Father's will and had to go through humiliation and suffering. Having taken up flesh to be like man on Earth, He had to undergo human disgrace for otherwise He could not have shown the world His unselfish sacrifice. With this act He left an everlasting impression on people. From the knowledge we have since we are here, it is not the idea that He atoned for the sins of humans. The real meaning of His sacrifice is misrepresented. Through His suffering He wished people on Earth to realise that unselfish love can do any sacrifice. Men on Earth make everything more elaborate than necessary.*

> *God knew that mankind was not asking for Him wholly and that if Christ came down He would have to go through some of the states of man. That is the only reason why we said: 'against His Father's will.'*

No one said He sinned through that action. An act under the impulse of love and help can never be looked upon as sin. It can be unwise to take a premature action and that is what happened and therefore we say He came down against His Father's wishes. The only mistake—if you can talk of a mistake—He did, was the impulse of giving light to mankind without possessing that wisdom which only God has. The Great One, as we said, knows no evil, no pain, sadness or misery, but His all penetrating light and His omnipotent wiseness knows exactly when men are ready to love implicitly. He knows when they turn towards Him and knows when they are looking for Him.

It is not in reality Christ's crucification or His resurrection, these do and have happened to others, it is His love which resembles most the love of God, which He left behind to mankind in ever growing waves of circles, that is helping humans and bettering them daily. Yes, my friends, it is that which is invisible to you, which is doing the work and not the false dogmas, upon which you lay your visible hands that represent Christ, the nearest to God.

Christ never understood evil. That is why He came down too soon and yet He will help man to regain absolute purity, but not until His words are rightly understood. As Christ came down before His time He had to go through the experience of man. Christ knew that He would be humiliated. At the same time He had no other intention but to reveal God to mankind and used the power He possessed up here, continually praising and loving God but also knowing that He could not—just like all humans cannot—avoid the penalties life on Earth brings with itself.

When Christ came down to Earth many seekers had visionary dreams about His arrival, so the news spread about.

We told you that very high up evil is unknown, and so it is, but remember Christ came down to Earth and mixed with evil and that on purpose, so as to understand what evil is, how it works and how it is best to purify the fallen, that is to say mankind. You know well enough that Christ could not be tempted and that His love and goodness was Divinity itself. It is the spirits, appointed by Himself and equally unable to be tempted, which are having the work of managing the *waves of evil and preventing them from doing absolute damage. Those spirits are the ones who see evil.*

The beloved Christ had to talk in parables because of the ignorance of men. The people could not have understood a simple disclosure. Simplicity requires highly educated souls, which now have arrived.

No dogmatic rule is the rule of Christ. The stories of the apostles are not used in the simple natural way of understanding, but Christ's words are given hidden meanings which certainly was not what He came down for.

Christ's message was too simple for the learned so they filled it with their own doctrine, blinding the innocent and simple ones.

Christ never forced anyone to follow Him, but they learned to feel for themselves and leading the pure life He did, He gave ideas to others to scrutinise themselves.

As Christ says about God: little goes far with my Father. That means that if you have started on the journey of goodness, great will your ultimate road be.

We told you that the Great One is order and law by His very nature and that being so all spirits ultimately return to Him. Do you follow this? You came from Him, to Him you return. This you do not, however, before you are absolutely pure. This is what Jesus Christ wanted you to understand mostly and that is why He came down to you and gave Himself to you and to the Great One.

You must not blind yourself by believing that as long as you believe that Jesus Christ cleaned and saved you by His supreme sacrifice you are guarded and all is well. That belief is, on the contrary, preventing you from the true vision that Jesus tried to reveal to you.

He spoke little and plainly, telling firmly the truth, the ways and modes of living, not minding sacrifices if it leads to purity. How many wish to interpret His message in that way? Mighty few, we tell you. It is easy to wash yourselves in the blood of the pure, but are they cleaner for it? Nay, that is not His message. He showed you the path that leads you to God, the path which is His, being the nearest to God, the path He wants you to follow, and by His crucification He intended to demonstrate that any sacrifice on your part is not big enough to cleanse you from the evil you allowed to enter your lives. This the meaning of true Christianity.

Now as to your question regarding the crucification, it would be incorrect to state definitely that the crucification was a special act for the redemption of souls. We can state, however, that all sacrifices ought to serve as examples for helping the purification, and that Jesus Christ's unique act stands out more powerfully and illuminating than any other, because from the very start of His life He was free from sin. In fact He represented the love-understanding of His Father of Whose very light He descended to Earth of His own free will. That is, of course, the difference between Him and the many others who also gave their lives for the sake of an example. What souls on Earth long for is Jesus Christ as He was and not as they made Him.

Despite the discrepancies in the Gospels, Jesus affected the disciples in a profound way, and we must believe that they were trying to paint as true a picture of Christ as they could describe.

The messengers inform us that they have seen the light of Christ from far away and that it helped them more than you can conceive.

We are told:

When once you have seen that, you cannot doubt any more. It is so wonderful that we are unable to describe it to you.

As they leave the subject of Christ, we are left with these intimate observations of His character:

Christ was an optimist to the last

and that He

is the picture of the complete idealist, who sees beauty and goodness everywhere,

though He,

the pure, condemned and used firmness towards the unjust and the hypocrite and rebuked the bad and wicked.

43

He possessed a subtle humor, but that was often misunderstood and therefore, absent in the Gospels.

> *Christ's eyes are the light of love and light. They penetrate into the depths of the part which is best in you and so He does His work with you.*

He is fond of children and

> *goes to those who left the Earth very young and them He teaches gently, lovingly. They learn from one of His visits more than from all your earthly life.*

The impulse to individual charity and the inspirations of idealistic thought are said to spring from His constant love for those who descended on Earth. Noble acts and thoughts, the messengers say, are influenced by the waves of Christ, which never cease to embrace the Earth.

Christ is also said to

> *rejoice in the love He receives from many on Earth and in the knowledge that He did good to all after all.*

Christ does not

> *communicate direct to Earth*

anymore, but

> *you can all feel Him.*

> *He sends a glow of warmth when you think of Him with pure love.*

> *Carry the Christ, who suffered the cross for you, in your heart and life's triviality will be no burden.*

> *Give yourself to the unseen but ever outstretched hands of Jesus Christ, the nearest to God, and you will live in the happiest of unspeakable joy.*

"If I have told you earthly things, and you do not believe, how shall you believe, if I tell you of heavenly things?"

— John, 3:12

7

HIGH MESSENGERS

There have been people throughout history who have generated revolutionary ideas from sudden inspiration. Some of these individuals who we call geniuses stand out in a category by themselves as being unique originators who created directly without building on others' works. We find them in all the main fields of human enterprise—in music, art, philosophy, and science. Their genius was interpretive but clearly creative, and they brought new agencies into progress on Earth. Were they—Socrates, Michelangelo, Beethoven, Pasteur, Edison, Einstein to name a few—divinely inspired to introduce their creations into our world? They were, so we are told. When humankind advances to a point where new ways of thinking can take root, certain individuals—blessed with their experiences from earlier incarnations—become receptive to divine influence.

We have been calling our spirit guides "messengers," but now we are to learn about special emissaries from the highest domains who the spirits call messengers. They are souls who have been sent from God to Earth, taking human form to live among humans and advance humankind's progress in all directions and regions of the world. We are told that these beings dwelled close to God and were living links between Earth and the highest spheres. Coming down from the vicinity of the Divine, like Christ, the foremost of God's messengers had to perform a special mission during a lifetime on Earth in the field where their own strongly developed individuality was rooted. Each arrived in our place with a definite purpose and reproduced patterns of beauty and activity which replicate the heavenly regions.

They descended because divine love compelled them to that personal sacrifice, and in their restless life of work, they gave humanity some glimpses of the world from which man had allowed himself to drift away. They created new impulses to raise the standard of life on Earth and aided in alleviating the burden we brought on ourselves by turning from the light of God.

As an aside, we are told that these emissaries have traveled from God's realm to other universes of His creation, that our Earth is not the sole province of God's attentions. The inhabitants of these other worlds, like us, have immortal souls seeking God's light and love. While this information is astonishing and even staggering to understand, we hear it announced matter-of-factly by the spirits, who as usual, are never surprised by our proclivity to believe we are unique. Earth and other places were originally designed for meditation to refocus and center the drifting souls, and they eventually became cleaning stations where souls could free themselves from the load which weighed them down, while the love of God followed them in their new existence. Unfortunately, the subject is not considered relevant to their work on Earth so we do not get detailed information on this fascinating concept.

God knows nothing of the pain and tribulations of man on Earth, but He is not aloof, nor does He decline to care for all His created beings. How could He, when a spark of Him dwells in each spirit and soul? Through displaying patterns of the heavenly beauty shown by His messengers He perpetually reminds us of the short duration of life on Earth and of the true nature of the eternal home.

The following messages will portray these emissaries, their genius, and the source of their inspiration.

Is it worthwhile to pursue philosophical studies? Are they as Socrates said: "the highest music?"

> *Philosophy is not known up here. That is the foundation of the brain. Socrates was not a philosopher in the sense you think of him on Earth. He was a high messenger who wished to show mankind the truth, but you see how difficult it is to understand a spirit who really dwells—even*

on Earth—on a higher step, so you can easily grasp how difficult it is for us to make you see conditions in which we live up here.

Was Plato then also a messenger?

Messengers are only the originators.

All those who gave humankind something quite new are messengers of the Great One. This refers to people like Buddha, Moses, Bach, Beethoven, Mozart, Rembrandt, Fra Angelico, Spinoza and quite a lot of others ever since souls descended to Earth.

Luther and Calvin?

No, Christ's teachings have been misunderstood by all.

And Dante D'Alighieri?

Dante was inspired by higher spirits, but he exaggerated the devil. No one is cast to eternal hell. Every soul is given a chance to better itself. The power of evil is not as strong as all that up here.

Why is Edison mentioned as a messenger? Others invented the wireless [radio].

There is always the originator and the mission of others is to better things.

The Great One lives far from men and even us in higher regions. He only lives with His messengers.

Is the duration of our lives on Earth the only thing which God decides? Does he not select the trials and the tests we have to undergo?

The Great One gets all information concerning man from the highest messengers and leaves the guiding of souls to them. Only the duration of their lives is decided by God, even if they have not fulfilled their lesson. In our spheres, however, a decision does not always correspond with time—time not existing here. The past is present and the present past, so it may happen that an event expected now does not take place as soon as we hoped. On the other hand it may happen sooner than expected. At any rate there are no great differences owing to those who can still calculate in earthly terms.

That souls who trust in God are not guided directly by Him may upset many of them because they feel uncertain of intermediaries.

> But, my children, can you not tell the world that the highest messengers are so near God that better guidance they cannot expect knowing that it is for denying God's absolute goodness that they had to become flesh. Do not imagine that you can come anywhere near God when you leave Earth. There will be innumerable stages of purification before you can even grasp the purity of the Great One.

> The messengers who dwelt on Earth come to help those on Earth and live up here for a long period with souls from Earth.

> The Great Almighty has allowed a few messengers to descend and give the lost but yearning souls a pattern of the beauties of art of various calibre and if you step aside from those patterns, whatever you may create will have no lasting value. It will vanish leaving no traces behind.

> There is only one God and there are many messengers unceasingly supplying mankind with inspirations and other things which mankind then improves and develops through their own free will, tolerance and perseverance.

> Nothing has been discovered on Earth that has not been invented up here by the Great One and His high messengers. Of course, we do not say that on Earth you have not the gift of inventing things, but it is a mighty few, if any, who have it, as the true world is only the world of the spiritual, as it is the only one which is everlasting, and on Earth everything originates from the world of truth.

But the mechanical inventions?

> Wait, do not rush at things. We had not ended our talk yet. We were just going to say that on Earth flesh has its needs, and so things are discovered for supplying those needs. The mechanical objects, mechanical conveyances, are all discovered by the necessity of needs for men, but we do not think that anything has been discovered without the influence of the Great One.

Was Plotinus[2] a messenger?

There are many of Plotinus's kind, very high thinkers, filled with wishes to help, endowed with great imagination, but he was not a messenger, as what he said was said by others.

Messengers are those who create on Earth a new view, new emotions which come to them from above and which none of them denied. Works, acts, resulting from intense use of the brain-system always under control, is not named messenger's work. They, men of Plotinus's type, are not working knowingly with waves like Christ, Moses, Buddha and Socrates.

Dear Friends, there are no single messengers working Earth now, but there is a vast number of very high souls about. You know and sense them easily. You will not find them moving in society or be with those who are out for novelties or sensations.

All great achievements are decided above and conveyed to those we call messengers—souls with the highest principles—specially sent down to communicate or create great examples from the highest spheres. You call them geniuses, a very inadequate expression, so easily misused. It is nothing of the kind. A genius can be given to the highest interpretative person, but that has nothing to do with what we call a messenger. It is a great achievement to be able to interpret great works, but the actual birth of great works or ideas comes from souls sent directly to Earth for the purpose

---

[2] **Plotinus** (AD 205-70), Roman philosopher, who founded Neoplatonism. Plotinus was born in Asyut, Egypt. Plotinus spoke on Pythagorean and Platonic wisdom and on asceticism. Plotinus continued to teach and write until his death. His works comprise 54 treatises in Greek, called the Enneads, 6 groups of 9 books each, an arrangement probably made by his student Porphyry (AD 232-c. 304), who edited his writings. Plotinus's system was based chiefly on Plato's theory of Ideas, but whereas Plato assumed archetypal Ideas to be the link between the supreme deity and the world of matter, Plotinus accepted a doctrine of emanation. This doctrine supposes the constant transmission of powers from the Absolute Being, or the One, to the creation through several agencies, the first of which is nous, or pure intelligence, whence flows the soul of the world; from this, in turn, flow the souls of humans and animals, and finally matter. Human beings thus belong to two worlds, that of the senses and that of pure intelligence. Inasmuch as matter is the cause of all evil, the object of life should be to escape the material world of the senses, and hence people should abandon all Earthly interests for those of intellectual meditation; by purification and by the exercise of thought people can gradually lift themselves to an intuition of the nous, and ultimately to a complete and ecstatic union with the One—that is, God. Plotinus claimed to have experienced this divine ecstasy on several occasions during his life.

of giving a taste of the realm of perfect beauty, which keeps its eternal source in the Great One, as we often said before.

All great creations—no matter whether material or spiritual—have originated in the world of the spirits and are conveyed to Earth by the spirits assigned.

We got your thoughts very clearly about the message referring to the messengers and their vicinity to the Great One. It is certainly badly expressed as no one but Christ has actually seen His Source. Christ is in that Source and therefore almost one with Him.

The others receive the light of the Great One in such a force that it enables them to act under direct communication and therefore we say that the messengers live near God, but we have never said—except for Christ—that they have seen God.

Of course, you must not imagine that there are no other great spirits than those you know about. Many dwell in other places and many have actually joined the Source of the Great One, but this cannot be grasped by you and for that you are not losing anything, as your and our work is only connected with Earth, one of the dwellings of unclean spirits.

How well we understand your surprise (that Christ is not the only one Who has joined the Source), yet does it not prove to you the limited imagination of mankind that they only saw Earth as a vital point in the universe? There are unnumerable worlds as the Great One never began and never will cease creating. That cannot happen with the Source eternal.

Feel this message; it will help you and also lessen the questioning thoughts which so many suffer from: How would it have been if we were never created? That thought was born from doubt and doubt was given by evil so as to upset perfect truth, trust in a Divine sense, harmony and joy and purity.

You may perhaps realise that even the messengers are not absolutely purified as—as long as you know of evil—you still have some left in you. This, however, must not worry you. One can be high and very good even if one fails a few times, but that is why one is not in the Source and this is in one respect necessary as only through it can we defeat evil on Earth.

"For what is it to die but to stand naked in the wind and to melt into the sun? And when the earth shall claim your limbs, then shall you truly dance."

— Kahlil Gibran

8

LIFE IN THE SPIRITS' DOMAIN

At this point in our spiritual education the messengers become more detailed in their descriptions and statements. Their improved capability to communicate their thoughts to the receivers is welcome because we are about to venture into the "everyday" life of spirits. The time is proper to learn about our messengers' quotidian activities because we are brimming with curiosity of the world beyond the veil, our ultimate destination.

What are you, spirits? You have told us you are sparks from God's eternal fire, endowed with individual qualities, free will, and the ability to progress and advance. You said we were once like you and carry that spark with us forever through our reincarnations on Earth, though we have little recollection of our previous lives. Can you revive our memory and explain more precisely what you really mean? Moreover, how do you and we differ? What do you look like–your shape and appearance? Are you the same personality as you were on Earth, and are you recognizable? How do you observe your new world? Does your world register time or contain space similar to ours? Are you confined to certain regions and periods, or are you free to move through the past and the future and through all the universe? Can you explain the nature of your pursuits, and do you have desires and aspirations? Do you have societies, laws, and rules which govern your lives?

These are a few of our questions we would like answered. All are not answerable; some are so bound to earthly conditions that there is nothing that corresponds to them on the other side. Time, the past, future, and space in their realm are particularly difficult to explain, but they try to enlighten us as best they can. Their comments are indeed beguiling and will challenge the reader's imagination to new heights.

As the communication sessions moved along, new spirit personalities drop in from time to time to elaborate on certain points. They are introduced as high spirits with greater knowledge than our regular messengers.

The messengers begin with shape, perception, and colors of the spirits.

Astral Bodies

You often wonder if one has a body up here and now perhaps you will more clearly understand when we say that we have a body up here, but not from flesh, which is material, but is a body of light in waves and in eternal harmony with the spirit which makes it work and not like on Earth, where the body makes or prevents the working of the soul.

The spirit, when it arrives up here, is like a light reflected by the sun. Its speed cannot be understood by man on Earth. It is practically everywhere simultaneously and is constant, not being associated with time.

The purer the spirit is, the brighter is the shine of the light that clads it.

The range of colour changes as we progress, the deeper the pastel—yet it must always remain clear—the higher the soul is.

Up here everyone is clothed in their own light, and it would be impossible to copy your fellow spirit as his garment is the outcome of his soul. No earthly garment can have the variety of each spirit up here, as their colours which are their clothes, scintillate in billions of colours according to the development of your feelings, etc.

Once you said that the speed of spirits is light.

But that is quite easy to grasp even on Earth. A spirit is not material, as you well know. It is neither a substance nor a liquid. It is something that never ceases to vibrate and is so swift that it can be everywhere almost simultaneously. Of course this refers to high spirits. Now that swiftness creates light, therefore we say that the speed of spirits is light.

It is not the kind of light you know, so that cannot be grasped. It is much more powerful and is a creative power.

Remember the word enlightenment descended from the high spheres, meaning the spirit getting lighter from reaching more light from the Great One, becoming more celestial.

Adjustments and Awareness

Is there anything comparable to death on Earth, when a spirit moves from one sphere to a higher?

No, for the spirit, once it is on the way of progress, there is no transformation of a similar kind, as that which you call death on Earth. There is naturally a change as it progresses, but you can always descend to your earlier stage and are not cut off like when a soul—the ever living—leaves the flesh. You become more transparent; your light acquires a brighter shine, a wider vibration which improves as you advance. The spirit is always recognisable once it is free from the body, contrary to Earth where always or nearly always you recognise the body, but hardly ever the soul or the spirit.

There is no reason why the spirit should undergo similar changes as when on Earth. The instant you recognise that your aim is towards the light of God, a metamorphose is not needed. What is life on Earth, what is a metamorphose? It is the hiding, the concealing of your true self as [compared to] when you enter the spirit life. We mean and talk of the spirits with true love in them. Well, when you enter that life there cannot be any concealment as you are drifting towards the real truth. We seem to emphasise this statement rather strongly, but we want to be absolutely clear and unhesitating about it.

Age

Once you get here, youth follows with you. Your spirit never ages, and instantly when you are here you regain the vigour of your soul. Have you not witnessed on Earth that the most decrepitated man or woman occasionally says the most brilliant and unexpected things? Well, that proves our statement.

Language

The pictures of the thoughts of the spirits are visible to the spirits, and they pass with each thought and can be compared to the language of humans.

Have you thought that when you speak into a microphone, your voice, although not touchable, not audible on its route in space—no matter the distance—can be and is heard at the place where it is expected to be heard? Well so it is with the spirit when it has left flesh. Where it is expected, it is felt, seen, and heard.

We do not talk in language, but in waves and coloured pictures. As thoughts do not come from the brain and so have to pass through the mouth, words are unnecessary. Therefore talking to you in words becomes extremely difficult to us.

Just as we on Earth receive messages from transcendent beings, they too receive communications from even higher spheres for their improvement. They say:

Just as you get messages from us, so we get them from higher mansions with the great difference that we know... We can believe in higher mansions even if we have not seen them yet. We know that one day we shall.

Sight of Earth

It is quite true that we can see you any time and at any moment.

How do you see us?

We see your spirit. From that the picture of your body. One lives in eternity with continual light and the complete absence of darkness.

Up here, we can see the past events on Earth much clearer than the historian. Up here, one gets the real events.

For us it is no difficulty to know any happenings on Earth; many are influences by us. The only errings we make is with time, but even there the difference is not great.

Any action of yours can be seen by us, but it is the thoughts that interest us.

Knowledge

One soon forgets the conditions when in flesh, just as you forget the cold when entering a hot country.

We learn and improve the whole time.

We get certain information from the ones above us.

We up here know a vastly many more things than you on Earth, as we are informed by the higher spirits. On that we form our individual opinion always shared by our spirit community up here. We live in love and brotherly bondage.

We can tell you what we ourselves know and that is far from ultimate knowledge.

There are numberless studies of various kinds. It takes perhaps one hundred earthly years to acquire a vision into the colouring of souls and so with everything. Ultimately, you master such complete knowledge in the life of the pure spirits that you are ready to dwell near the Great One. To feel the smallest part of His light gives you eternal glory, and then you know what God is.

After one arrives here, the truth shines in its purest garment. We are not groping in the dark, taking chances whether this or that view will enable us to impart a clearer picture of what we believe was a perfectly justified argument. Up here, we progress unceasingly. There is no point of arguing. You cannot discuss with the light and love of God; you [take it in] to make you advance further.

Spirits from higher spheres descend to give illumination about the perfect love and so it goes on progressing as they learn.

Man's and spirit's aim through the influence of the highest is a continual progress.

We all have a common aim and that is to please the Great One. We have an absolutely different idea of values and arguments and different opinions do not come into question. Here we see the heavenly perfection in every value and do not search for absolute values as on Earth. You also see the thoughts of all spirits, so where is room for different opinions?

We have only one desire: to work for attaining that perfection of values which is revealed in those patterns.

In the realm of spirits, there exists an absolute lack of argument and progress is made for the sake of progress without any comparison. Freedom of action is wholly individual, thus, true advancement takes place.

Thoughts become actions and alive; therefore, discussions would be wasted here. One must find the road by oneself and no other spirit can do that for one.

On Earth, the greater part of one's life is wasted by discussions and the desire to find out why [something] has happened instead of doing one's own work. Only individual work can truly progress—that we soon realise up here.

We, too, have graduations in our advancement. We, too, have to learn and our lessons are far more difficult. The brain limits your faculties, but here knowledge is limitless and with love as its brother, weds us to the eternal wish for ultimately joining the circle of God.

Free will up here is really to improve your individuality, [while] on Earth [its] to choose between good and evil. No one is forced to love up here, but in our spheres it becomes the natural route to take.

Once you leave flesh and become a spirit, the real is unclad and you know from whom to guard yourself. Spirit life is free from being blind for those who are your enemies. Our enemies are not in our community, but follow the regions of evil. Therefore, we can work more freely than you on Earth, who more or less grope in the dark. Up here we do not live in any contact with evil. On Earth, good and evil are closely together. Therefore one advances steadily towards the light of God, which continually cleanses all defects of the past in us not by will or force, but by the natural flow of His love and innocence.

Up here, opinions, statements, feelings, ideas, inventions, tastes, and most of all love must be and is absolutely decisive and without hesitation and of one thought.

In the actual spirit world, advanced in stages, there is no sorrow, and we can only find sorrow when men on Earth are concerned. We live in such a perfect harmony that sorrow, envy, bad humour cannot come in question. We could not approach those with innocence with statements which are not existing there. Gloom and sadness is unknown in the very highest spheres and likely to cast a mist on the waves. That is the beauty of those high ones, my son, pure like crystal water. You would not want that kind of water to be soiled and would do all to keep its purity.

Spirits do not need air; flowers do not need soil up here. You see them whenever you want and then walk amongst them. You do not walk like on Earth, yet you walk. The flowers do not grow out of the soil, yet they bloom as if from a root. Up here, flowers love you, like you love them on Earth. They feel and follow you on your voyages. Up here, the imagination is a true thing and is living, so you can experience everything in your imagination. When your spirit arrives up here, the imagination—which in a relaxed state on Earth makes you see all kinds of things, past, present and future, passing like a wind—becomes truth and active.

Up here, there is no superiority feeling, and our being higher up comes as a matter of course.

Up here, you must not expect honours or bowings for your work on Earth. If it were that you hoped for, you would be greatly disappointed. On the other hand, expect love, peace, harmony, and brotherhood. If you can give your life into such conditions, you can start an existence on Earth similar to our life.

We up here do not expect what you do on Earth and in consequence, we are happier and if we see love, that is all we want. Were we to live up here wondering of what others think of us, we should show up a poor picture. Here that sort of thing does not exist, as thoughts are known to all. We are not judging matters from the aspect of ears, eyes, and senses, but from the light which carries our spirit along the road of God. The life of spirits—or rather the spirits—is the material which is drawn by the magnet which is God himself. Only those with His love and light can and are drawn to Him.

Law

Order and organization exists but not like on Earth. There, obedience is one of the greatest laws, as it is the light of God they are serving. On Earth, law is forced upon us; there, it is salvation. The desire to follow the light of God can only be reached through patience, order, and absolute tolerance.

In the sphere of souls, love rules and love that comes from the Great One knows no ambition, envy or jealousy, but wishes to give and serve without limitation.

You do not wish to rule up here: you rest in love and live in accumulating wisdom.

Spirits have power, but that cannot be compared to earthly power, which is used mostly for one's self, whilst power of heaven means giving love and compassion to those lower or higher spirits. You do not wish to rule up here: you rest in love and live in accumulating wisdom.

Up here, we help each other continually. We have no feeling of degradation. We know that we shall possess the greatness of God and never wish for it. One is a servant of the Great One, but none of us could ever work as He does.

Here, law is in you, and you do not know about it. The heavenly sphere is a law by itself, not born from anything, but always was; everything good is born from it.

The world of truth—that is the world of the spirits—is so organised and so minutely calculated that everything has its place, work, etc. Remember that it is the world of the Great One.

The greatest beauty and joy up here will be the simplicity of matters. We are like magnets. The ones with the same substance in waves are drawn to each other. Waves containing different lights to ours make the magnetism dead and the waves never meet.

All you see on Earth has its real home up here, living in eternal bloom and fragrance. What you see is only a fraction of a sample God created to delight poor sinners. The spirit never tires of beauty.

Space

We can travel anywhere and in a speed you cannot conceive, but we cannot yet go up where the Great One lives. The light around Him is too pure for us.

The speed of spirits cannot be surpassed by anything.

Well, good friend, easy it is not to grasp the spheres of the spirits whilst on Earth, but after you arrive up here, you soon realise that this is truth and earthly life more or less an illusion, built up from faint recollections. You are correct when you say that if time stops, space stops also, right in the point of view of the physical world, as that works together, but here we have order which is omnipotent as it is directly emanating from God. In our view, there is space up here, but we cannot call it that, as we reach anywhere at any second, speaking your language.

On your arrival up here. Why 'up' here? We always use that word which is not really correct. Around, about, indivisional section, is better than the above. There is no above nor below in the world of truth. Space combines all, yet space has–like existence–no end and no beginning. Beloved, you know that we can reach you no matter how far we are. That is because in the spirit life, there is no space nor time. Yes, for you it exists, but with us those calculations are different. The spirit is faster than space or time. Can you grasp this? The end is the Great One, but as no one can reach there, we continually move on. We see that this will not be understood and any clearer explanation is futile as we have no calculations, as you on Earth.

Spirits up here are space. Believe it so and the space we are, or form, or occupy, is dependent on the purity of our spirits and their progress. Remember the Great One combines the whole, and that means all the space, so as we are His sparks, we are space, too, but it is no use to try to clear up something which is essentially part of celestial existence. If you try to explain to a small child some philosophical problem, it–as you well know–cannot understand anything about it, and yet it is flesh talking to flesh. You are in one respect as unlearned as the child, but once you arrive here, your true spirit existence recollects all that is mystery to flesh.

Time

Time in the sense that we know it does not exist in the domain of spirits. Yet, they have a kind of regulated movement that, though nothing to do with time, gives a sensation of events coming and going. Everything changes but retains all the past and present and also a great part of the future. Even on Earth there is in one respect no time. The moment a word is spoken, it is past, and yet it is present. Beyond the veil, they measure duration in events and emotions, not in the mechanical movement of a sun.

Up here, the pendulum ceases to move, yet you will progress forever.

Here, everything is outside time, having no end and no beginning.

Time is non-existent here, and all is like a second in comparison with the longest life on Earth.

We have no time here and find it difficult to realise it ourselves. The complete absence of time is for ascending spirits a most difficult thing. We are on the move constantly, yet we do not know it. We can look at the past just as at the future, though only in picture form, and only endless studies enable us to ascertain which is which in the past and future.

Do you see events coming like we feel it in a dream?

Not quite in the same way, but there is certainly a resemblance because our world does not register through a brain, nor do we see with earthly eyes; what is to you coming in a dream is to us reality with the reservation, of course, that the pictures are not always in the same clear appearance. If the picture is very much encircled by evil, it becomes less clear to us who are aiming upwards to the light of truth. It is not so easy to grasp as you think or imagine.

Eternity is before you...

It is also behind us, here and now, and coming?

No, it is before you, as once you descended to Earth, time starts, and time is not eternal. Time is outside the eternal circle. When you descend to Earth, you leave eternity behind and something new and different enters your soul. Of course, this is only a temporary condition, yet important to a degree.

Even on Earth, time is an illusion. Were time the value you attribute to it, the past would stand out, cut out in sections. In reality it has no importance whether a thing happened one year, ten years, or a hundred years ago. Once past, it cannot be retrieved by you. But to us, the past is present, just like the future is always there. We advance, remain stationary or fall back, though always in the circle which is outside Earth and so has no time, but advances in itself.

Time is an earthly arrangement and cannot come in question with eternity. Through pictures, we appreciate the duration of human life, but that is not fixed. This a mathematical illusion.

Though you have no measurement of the sequence of events, you must, so we think, have an impression of a sequence?

Up here, there is no past, present or future in [significance] to consecutive time of events. You judge by Earth, ruled by time, but remember our work is totally different to yours, though we help all continually. But that has no connection with our own work. Beloved friend, it is so hard to explain all this, because on Earth you want concrete facts and cannot live or grasp the waves of the celestial.

We have told you there is no time in the way you know it, but there is something else which is continuous and which we cannot explain or be understood by those who work and live in the flesh. If you think that one goes by pictures, it may give you a new idea of how we have it. Again we do not see pictures, as you do on Earth, but visualise your own spiritual or—as you say—mental pictures.

How strange to speak of the future which is so essentially earthly. Up here, we do not talk of future because events are continuous. The word 'future' belongs to the world where time exists.

But you have a sequence of events?

Yes, but that has nothing to do with time. The way we work, we always know where it will lead us. Also, jumping from one thing to another does not exist with us. We told you there is no time like yours on Earth, but we all have to reach His light. There everything stops, only to develop in oneself.

Activities

When the souls arrive up here, they are after a while shown what their spirits will have to do.

When the soul leaves the body, the desires change.

Life here is a constant occupation. We have no flesh, so there is no need for food, and in consequence no time is wasted on such matters. If we wish for a distraction, we can hear music of a kind you get only glimpses of on Earth and poetry more divine than you can conceive. Politics, finance, money have no place here.

Nothing is an effort here.

Our work is continually inspired by love, and you could not understand it as long as you are in the flesh.

Spirit life is full of activity, and everyone has a special work to do.

Your love for any sort of art remains with you forever, and up here develops to a much higher form. Likings for earthly amusements, if you are a spirit that raised to great heights whilst on Earth, in time lose their attraction and you live only for love, charity, and beauty.

What flow of melodies, what golden rhymes here. Your soul will be submerged in glory, which is of a quality inexplicable to souls on Earth. All have to go through gradual lessons. For them, do not get anxious. You are closely helped by all good spirits once you get here.

Your inventive power is the action of your spirit and knows the capacity of your abilities, and as everyone is an individual spirit and works in that line, there cannot be a conflict between spirits, and everyone goes on in his progress. Of course, this refers to spirits in such spheres where goodness prevails. With those under the power of evil, things are dark and in a chaos to our aspect.

Everything on Earth, though great, is but a minute fraction of the wonders you shall see and by and by achieve yourself. All on Earth is a preparation for the real work that is awaiting you on your arrival. The creations on Earth are only small divertissements to make men realise what they can expect.

We spirits have an enormous work, as it is for us to manage man on Earth. God has given all a breath of His divine love and free will to man to manage his own life, leaving them to themselves and the supervision of them to us.

The work of purification is left to man, guided—if listened to—by high spirits, who watch over each soul.

We, who are anxious for the world to get the truth, enter the studies which enable us to manipulate the waves in such a fashion that you on Earth can receive them and know that they come from us.

There is a countercreation against all evil, but as that is managed by high messengers, it is not an infallible work. God could not counteract, as He knows no evil. The high spirits have much to do with the management of the souls on Earth. We cannot create the minutest life and we can never give colour to things, but we are the voluntary servants of that God, Who is love and light and are participating in the manipulation of waves in every respect.

Much in the universe is controlled by high spirits.

The Great One has many near Him, doing the work he gives them. Spirits, who are very high and are the messengers of God, have individual creative power, as far as inventions are concerned and have their own ideas. The vital power of creating spirits and light is not given to them, as only God creates without His knowledge and emanates light the same way.

Up here, we are enveloped in a joyful attitude. On Earth, things do not quite correspond with the spirit world. On Earth, one is so dependent on the body and various circumstances, and where one does not see the thought of others, it becomes more difficult to operate and act. Up here, in our community, one has already reached a level where petty events do not exist. We live for progress and embrace all who are on the same journey. When you reach our spheres, you do not waste your energy, your thoughts—or rather your feelings—on the destruction of others, but you carry on with your work with only one object that is: together advance to the light of the purest love.

Inspiration from God to men is sent through the spirits from the higher regions. We receive them and send them to you.

There are those from higher regions whose power has more strength than ours, and where we stop, they continue. Our essential duty is to fill you with continual and fresh inspiration, sent to us by higher powers. You are the venues through which God will conquer evil.

When Swedenborg talks as if angels—or what we call spirits—would not know of conditions on Earth, he is wrong. We are aware of the beliefs and disbeliefs of souls on Earth and that is why we try to communicate with them, so as to give them the right impression. We are all working up here for the salvation of man.

Though we live in a higher sphere, surrounded by beauty and light, we cannot always feel inspired in the same way. We never get tired, but are not machines, and sometimes we are more interested than other times.

It is extremely difficult to make you understand the work of the spirits, which is essentially outside any wish of personal glory. When developed enough, it works and creates for the sake of creating and not from ambition. We have told you often that ambitions belong to Earth.

There will always be a number of limitations in clearing certain mysteries, working between Earth and the world of the spirits, as one is based on a mechanical routine and recurrences, whilst the other works in the emotions of the spirit and is as varied as the size of the stars and never recurs. Our life, though moving in order, is a constant advance; no repetition occurs. We must go on in the advance towards the circle, and that is something utterly different to what you aim at on Earth.

Each individual spirit is a spark of God and, if that is so, as we know it to be, it must be that each spirit is an individuality in a lesser or bigger sense of the word. Follow the work, the doings of mankind on Earth. That which is done by hand, by the mind, is never twice the same, because it is the spirit part which is unceasingly changing and makes the work just as nature, music, varies and is never the same. Things on Earth that are the same can only come from the use of machinery. Unless the Great One would not be a continual living force of love, beauty, and goodness, he would also produce spirits which would be mechanical and which could not be elastic. Every thing living containing elasticity must be variable.

Waves

The whole real existence is living by waves. The subtle, invisible work of the wave system cannot yet be understood by mankind.

The thought creates waves. Every emotion has its circular wave.

The wireless communication is the nearest to what we have up here. We can gather waves to us whenever we want and can transform them to any length.

We have every possible range of lights and are receiving powers which we can manipulate in various ways, whilst on Earth you are handicapped by long and short wave-lengths, and one wave interferes with the other.

The spirits have a different kind of wave according to the work they have to do.

The higher you dwell, the quicker the waves move, as they wish to reach multitudes.

We shoot out waves from ourselves and, thus, spread a light which we cannot see but which is doing valuable work to mankind.

Events are waves approaching us.

You receive waves which influence you from the world of the spirits, yet we realise that scientists would like to interpret this in another fashion.

The waves we speak of cannot be registered by machines and differ from such waves. They are spiritual and find contact with the spiritually sensitive.

The working, the interweaving of waves is so delicate, so pure, that the slightest disturbance upsets their work.

The waves are yourself and ever varying, just as with Him, who kissed the spirit of each of you, is a continual variation.

Regions

Does it not seem an absurd nonsense that you after death go either to heaven or hell? Can you picture a person, although noble in thought, but absolutely unlearned, to be at once by the side of God? Do you not recollect the words of Christ: 'in my Father's place there are many mansions?' Do you not recollect Buddha saying 'you go higher and higher until you are lost?' That meant to go through innumerable stages, until you can lose yourself. It means absolute purification, not annihilation, and so you become nameless.

When Christ speaks of mansions, it means stages of spiritual development of each spirit who is ready to enter the first mansion. Those mansions do not receive bad souls who listened to evil. They remain near Earth.

Spirits cannot at once reach the highest spheres. They must learn a lot before that. There are, even in love, different scales and until you are entirely purified, you must go through many stages, but bear in mind that the lessons are not toilsome, but a great joy and happiness which on Earth is marred by the difficulty to keep evil's influence checked.

It is very much how you live and think on Earth that you will continue up here, which must be logical to you.

The soul, becoming spirit, if evil, cannot face the light of the Great One; hence–after the body has been cast off–takes a different road to the good spirits. It is your doing and not God's, Who knows only light and love.

With what you learnt on Earth, you advance into the eternal wishing to better yourself continually, never stopping in your energy, which is indefatigable once you have no longer a body.

Those on Earth, who sink lower, once they lose their bodies, according to the law of spirits and as a natural cause, are obliged to go through a more severe test than that in Earth.

Your souls are, of course, immortal, but many refuse accepting Him and those live near Earth and are liable to return to Earth.

There are graduated regions according to how much one believed in the power of love, how genuine your wish to do good or wished good for other fellow men, for those who realised that man can never reach perfection, for those who lived for success only, for those who are wishing evil and nursed hatred in their hearts, and many others. Those different regions we call mansions for the understanding of mankind. We cannot describe more as it would convey nothing to you. All we can say is that the higher you go, the more magnificent it becomes.

There is a light of such power that it blinds earthly eyes. There are flowers ever blooming, as here everything lives in thought forever. Scent and beauty envelop all in the higher regions.

If you lived on Earth with a desire to feel God and dwell in thoughts more for the future life, you will find it very easy up here and a great relief to find that all cares concerning the body and everything which goes with it is left behind and that which we take up with us can shine by the love of God and the love you brought up with you. If, however, we bring with us all the desires and ambitions we had on Earth, it will take a long period before we can settle down and accept the idea of constant work for others. Those souls go to a coma and so half asleep try to live or rather continue their earthly lives.

Blue is the colour of the first stages of the spirits. Beyond that you get other colours. It is what you would call a permanent discharge of electricity, though for us it is a different condition and not explicable in words. Up here, emotions, feelings, and other such [expressions] have all colour and the magnitude of the colour varies according to the strength of the conditions. Many things will and must puzzle you as spirit conditions do not resemble conditions on Earth.

The blue you see does not actually represent the spirits, just like the rays of the sun are not actually the sun itself but shoot out from it. Exactly the same happens with the discharge of spirits. What you see is the coloured rays or carpet of the spirits. The spirits of the blue spheres are the ones nearest Earth.

Were you to see with the spirit, you would be astounded to find that you are surrounded by them, some old, some young, who cannot raise higher. The desire of Earth pulls them. Those are around you.

Communities

There are innumerable communities for all souls. For those who never left the heavenly spheres, they are joined with those who were messengers on Earth and there are different regions until you come so near His light that you become part of Him, having lost any other desire but beauty clad in his light. It is a long pilgrimage.

When we talk of communities, it does not mean that we are all on the same level, but that the essential, which is love, is equally accepted and recognised by everyone. On Earth, you also are drawn to those who feel with you. They may differ greatly in knowledge, some more advanced than yourself, yet the essentials are shared, and so it is up here with the difference that thoughts are seen so you cannot be taken in.

Here, we do not retain nationality, but join the big community whose sole interest is for the Great One and has no personal aim.

Races are all together. The colour distinction of races remains in thought only. Nations naturally have no interest.

Our community consists of all earthly nations and of various periods. Spirits from higher spheres communicate with us just as you do, with the difference that we know they are true.

The communities are not rigid; on the contrary all is elastic up here. Snobbishness and ambitions are nonexisting. Life is not comparable to that on Earth. Of course, we talk of those who have lost earthly desires and are driving in the love for Him higher and higher.

Many of our communities improve in purity quicker than others and, thus, go higher, but we never lose touch with them; on the contrary, we receive more illuminating instructions ourselves.

It may happen that we go down to lower regions; we often do, but seldom get followers as they prefer to continue a life more like on Earth, which the nearer Earth you are the easier you can do. Ultimately, nearly all change, but by that period you are so high up that your desires are only for God, and family ties are nowhere. That is only an earthly episode.

Because we live in communities, do not imagine that we have alien feelings for those who live in others. We are all working for one and the same Master. The whole system up here is so different for those who believe in the Great One's absolute purity.

You can be alone up here, but, curiously enough for you on Earth, after you arrive up here, you do not wish to be alone, and that desire completely vanishes after a period. Here, there is no hiding, for those who are pure as the thoughts are open to all.

You see, all the conditions change the instant you leave the body behind. Ministers, rulers, clergymen, etc., are not necessary for us spirits. We follow the light and so progress.

"Angels are spirits, but it is not because they are spirits that they are angels. They become angels when they are sent. For the name angel refers to their office, not their nature. You ask the name of this nature, it is spirit; you ask its office, it is that of an Angel, which is a messenger."

— St. Augustine

9

THE NAMELESS

On occasions, during the periods of communication with the spirit messengers, high spirits of a distinct character appeared. They would make their presence known, state truths of special significance, and end their messages with a sign of unique recognition. They called themselves "The Nameless."

We have no name. We serve Him Who is one and all in good.

The regular messengers later elaborated and described these beings in greater detail:

They are those who have no name, for those who have names and have lost all ambitious desires and are only wanting to help in the wisest way.

The Nameless are angels, spirits who have never been down and light shines through them continually. They come and go among all the communities, bringing joy and wisdom wherever they go. They are highly individual, highly inventive, but their knowledge they use for the benefit of others and not for their own welfare. Remember they never left His light, which gives the supreme happiness of forgetting oneself, the only true joy existing and, once possessed, leaves nothing to desire, yet vibrates in everlasting bliss.

The Nameless explained their mission and special work for the people of Earth:

The happiness of others is our glory.

It is our work and mission to inspire on gentle lines always in the expectation that the free will of man—of which he is the sole master—can be influenced by other wills. Failing this, however, firmness must be the other attitude.

Children of Earth, be noble. Think little of yourself. Live in the thought of putting yourself out for your fellow men. The more uncomfortable the better for your improvement. Learn to forget the word 'I' in every respect, then you will be more ready for the life of light.

We, the Nameless, know that evil is the strong on Earth and can divert waves from catching the circle of God.

Resist all his moods and victory will be yours.

There is chaos in Earth. Men begin to understand that earthly leaders drag them to misery; hence, we tell you, men are ready to surrender to the one and only Master, Whom to serve means whitening their souls, and Who gives them the heat which keeps them in eternal bliss and willing activities. Never let yourself be disturbed by the wicked tongue of evil.

You must learn to live in contentment and so draw to yourself waves of the same order. Remember that like attracts like.

True belief never fails to receive its fruit.

The Nameless speak of guardians, angels who work exclusively with souls on Earth to encourage, warn, protect, and influence our free will for the advancement of our journey toward the light of God.

The guardians are spirits who never descended to Earth and are called angels there.

Every soul on Earth has the corresponding spirit up here who tries to help. We cannot help all, but are at the same time ready to help those outside our sphere, as we long to help.

Each spirit is individual and its guardian is more or less of the same nature as itself without, of course, any evil. It would be useless, for example, for a very low person to have a spirit like Socrates to watch over him and to send him influencing waves. An educated person, on the other hand, is capable of learning from vastly superior voices, emanating from a messenger guardian.

Up here, where personal ambitions are not in existence, all appointments of guardians are without personal bias and we all know how fit we are for certain undertakings; after harmonious meetings, we decide who of us are most appropriate to stand by earthly beings and so we try our best to use our influential waves. In the case of deciding who shall guard the individuals on Earth, the communities decide and man receives the waves from the same guardian all through life.

Those in the high spheres perceive the waves of human thought and emotion as flowing slowly, as in a slow-motion film. Their own waves are very swift and influential and have ample time to intervene, but we are told that this contrasting velocity makes it difficult for us to sense their flashes of advice and follow the intended influence. It seems that our biological construction, mainly our brains and the random cacophony of our self-chatter, blocks the spiritual emanations. The spirits suggest meditation and quiet periods of reflection to help assimilate and profit from their beneficial radiations.

"No evil dooms us hopelessly except the evil we love, and desire to continue in, and make no effort to escape from."

— George Eliot

10
EVIL

In prior communications, the messengers have spoken repeatedly of the conflict, degradation, and damage evil has done and continues to wreak upon earthly souls. In fact, they have told us that our primary task on Earth is to overcome and defeat evil. We are here because evil tainted our souls. Evil's desire is to hurt, damage, destroy, and prevent God's creation from following His light. It is the most singular and profound problem we on Earth must solve, per the teachings which follow.

But what is evil? There are many who do not believe evil exists, at least not as a separate force or entity. Others believe that evil is necessary for us to recognize good, and that, therefore, evil can co-exist with good. Others turn the issue over to science and its doctrines, believing that science will identify, explain, and "inoculate" society from evil's manifestations with little effort from us. Look at the many diseases that have been "cured" by the application of scientific principles. These individuals will point to the improvement in our quality of life, our longevity, and the standard of living we enjoy, and are willing to credit science fully. All we must do is give the researchers more time and money, and we can be free of all things bad, they assert.

These are level-headed, rational people who can be quite vociferous in their annoyance with any of our attempts to find answers through faith and intangibles not measurable by instruments. Their philosophy is, "I'll believe it when I see it." Morality is relative.

Science in its objective, rational, measurable, predictable, irrefutable logic, however, has not been able yet (and never will) provide the cure for evil. By definition, then, it will not provide the answer to the meaning of life. Our lives are of spirit. Without the breath of God, the body would be an unanimated, comatose-like organism. Without a soul, we are nothing more than a complex chemical-electrical mechanism. But this is what the scientists study: our biological, chemical functions. The advances are simply the result of figuring out how a specific system, organ, or another bodily part runs. Then a method, drug, or device is formulated to repair the problem.

Yet, despite all the sophisticated mechanical repair effort, when a patient dies, the death confirmed by medical instruments, sometimes the unmeasurable occurs—a patient returns from death. Many times, these people have had a life-altering experience and report with awe their contact with life after death. From what we have learned here so far, we should not doubt the accounts, even though the experiences are scoffed at by the experts as nothing more than the dying brain firing electrical impulses in response to oxygen deprivation and release of chemical discharges as it winds down. The experiences cannot be proved, e.g., measured or detected by our tools and devices—therefore the event did not occur.

The patient is patted on the back and treated as an embarrassment. They soon learn not to discuss the experience with anyone but their closest friends. The near-death experience is but one example of the failure of science to seek answers to the fundamental mystery of life: Who are we? Why are we here? Where are we going? And if the scholarly disciplines cannot overcome their institutional skepticism and arrogant dismissal of anything spiritual, how can they be relied upon to defeat evil, which is a dark spiritual force we must conquer to leave this Earth plane forever?

Much time is devoted to the discussion of evil in the next several pages. The spirits take evil's influence very seriously. They also leave no doubt that it is up to us individually exercising our free will to carry out this herculean task. But before we can, we must understand all guises, schemes, and artifices that evil invokes to avert our ascendancy into the heavenly realms.

The messages are not pleasant reading. We will learn the truth of evil's influence and the powerful force we must defeat. Yet, they offer hope in their firm conviction that evil will be eradicated. It is simply a matter of time since the natural direction of God's sparks is toward the good. How much time is up to us and our willingness to join the battle in earnest.

Humans are comparable to a drug addict with a lethal habit who deep down knows that the addiction and continued life are incompatible, that at some point a choice between the drug or life must be made. Like us, the addict realizes that a decision is inevitable but tries to delay the effort as long as possible, hoping that somehow, tomorrow maybe, change will need no sacrifice, no struggle. The longer they hesitate, the greater the likelihood that they will not alter their lifestyle and will die in an alcoholic or drugged haze.

Like the addict, we are at the crossroads—not of physical deterioration from a chemical, but of spiritual decline from ignorance of our spiritual legacy. The messengers aspire to rectify this shortcoming and persuade us to use our gift of free will to choose life in God's light.

To understand evil, it is helpful first to review traditional philosophy and prevalent beliefs on the nature of evil. This is not a modern debate; it has been ongoing for eons. Plotinus equated matter with evil. Contemporary intellectuals agree with Plotinus, arguing that evil is an attribute of nature. They assert that nature carries the evil in itself and a conflict is going on between spirit and matter, and matter is the "lowest stage of being." Since man is matter, man is inherently evil. Yet this view does not agree with common sense and our own observations. Nature can be destructive and violent, but also peaceful, beautiful, and soul-satisfying. Why must evil be in nature when, like humans, there are good and bad examples of both in our experience?

It has been said that no other evil exists in reality but that which is recognized by man as evil and is rooted in the individual appreciation of values. Many theologians searched for the origin of evil in the self. But anyone who has struggled hard for their betterment, quietly searching their soul in the hour of temptation, are not satisfied with this explanation. It does not cover the actual process during moral conflicts in our lives. Having conscientiously watched our inner state of mind, we become aware of a battle waged between an attraction towards good and something opposing our wish to reach it. Listening carefully, we hear voices, whispering or loudly speaking, emotionally driving us one way or the other, announcing opposite directions, tendering advices, injecting doubts and stoking our emotions.

This is a puzzling experience which many good and moral individuals have undergone. Reflecting on the conflict, we realize that living factors work within us, opposing forces vying for our acceptance. Gradually, we can see that there are defining characteristics separating the forces and this leads to a resolution of the two camps, allowing us to resist evil's enticements more easily.

According to the messages, the battle is not between a lower and a higher self, as Jung and others have concluded. In a healthy human, the ego is a single unit and fully aware of the forces, making its choice between the opposing factions. It is not the "I" which first comes into action, but forces impress themselves upon the self, and the decision follows. Satisfaction and peace are reached, not through theoretical reasoning, but through yielding to the influence which inspires good.

As mentioned earlier, there is a body of thought that believes that good cannot be distinguished clearly except through experiencing its opposite. According to this idea, evil becomes a teacher, instructing man on the nature of good. The messengers will begin their comments with a refutation of this notion. This concept would mean that it is essential to possess knowledge of evil for the appreciation of good, and that purification of souls is only possible through a confrontation with the bad. It is a paradoxical position which smacks of relativism: evil in another is good for us in disguise.

As we have seen, the concept of waves is woven throughout the explanations of God's influence, the spirits' perception of earthly happenings and their contact with us. When they describe life in the spirit world, they refer to waves as the fundamental aspect of their essence and the world they inhabit. Evil exerts its influence and accomplishes its goals through the force of waves, using them to block and interfere with those emanating from the higher spheres. We can now see that the problem of evil is removed from matter and nature into the intangible world of the spirit, which is all there is.

So now let us begin our education about evil with the spirits' reply to the false belief that evil exists to make us aware of good, and therefore, is necessary for man's spiritual progress.

We take up the dialogue at the point where the spirits have listened in on the receivers' discussion of good and evil:

> *We are amongst the best of souls, but there is one point we do not agree with and that is your view on the necessity of evil for progress. Put your argument forward.*

Progress advances from the lower towards the higher, until perfection is reached, evil being the lowest stage.

> *We cannot agree with you on this question. Let us see. You say: evil must exist or else progress cannot take place. What about the bud? Does it not grow into a flower in time? Is that not progress in beauty?*

> *You are all far too much engrossed in the idea of the necessity for opposites for sure progress. This is the stamp of evil even in the best of you. This stamp you will never find in Jesus Christ and His messages. Look upon the perfection of the Great One perfecting itself.*

> *Men ought to understand that evil is the preventer of progress. If your argument admits that good can become better, we shall stand by you, but do not—even for the sake of discussion—give any place for justifying the existence of evil.*

Later, in a similar discussion among themselves, the recipients had written a note saying that suffering and conquering of obstacles might be necessary for the functioning of the cleaning station of souls called Earth. Although the question was never actually posed, an answer arrived saying:

> *Your question is not easy to answer because the sole object of souls descending into a body is due to the reason of having listened to the temptation of evil, and if evil would not exist, bodily existence would not have been necessary. At the same time, we absolutely refuse the theory that evil is necessary for progress and maintain that it can only destroy ultimately, even if for a while it seems to the contrary to you. Of course, to you it seems essential to know of evil to combat that force and acquire the very opposite for progress in a good sense. Here comes the difficulty in answering your question as, whatever we say, the fact remains that having been born and lived surrounded with evil elements, you cannot absolutely wipe out that force and its influence follows you on every path.*

It does not necessarily mean that you are evil, but your conceptions on morals and attributes are bound to be measured on a basis influenced by conditions thus existing.

What can we do, but to say that if you come, as you do, from God, and God does not know evil—as if He would, He could not be God—then how is it necessary to know evil for progress? Follow the progress on Earth and you will soon discover that unless you are free from evil influence, you will fall back to the same mistakes as your ancestors did. This to us is enough proof that—contrary to your conceptions—evil only teaches you renewed mistakes. The greatest progress has only been achieved by those who knew no evil at heart. Good is only good if it stands alone. The moment it is good, because it wants to be opposite to bad, it does not stand alone. Can you understand this?

On re-reading the original question the spiritually sensitive heard the following:

We carry within us that evil to Earth. It is not so that we first meet evil on Earth.

Did the sensitive correctly grasp this direct communication?

Of course. She seldom 'hears' wrong. This is how we like to work.

We have been discussing how we could make mankind understand in the simplest way the reason of earthly life, its connection with evil and the Great One. Why do you all bore so much into 'how and why' when by now everyone ought to know that to come to Earth means that one has sinned and that one must learn to get purified through one's own conviction and one's own inner voice.

Life on Earth has many beauties. These beauties have been created to enable mankind to see purity in purity so that there is no question that ugliness is necessary for appreciating beauty. This is one point, simple but vital, which, however, is omitted by those boring into the mysteries of life on Earth. It is the simplicity which does not interest those who spend their energy on discovering the object of earthly existence.

Now, if, as we said, nature is created to show beauty and to progress that beauty, why the doctrine of evil being necessary for progress?

Cannot you see that? There are many other examples, but it is not necessary to mention them just yet.

We said that nature in its splendour has been created to enable mankind to progress in beauty and it is open to all—poor and rich—which again is another proof that the Great One does not know suffering. But here comes the work of evil, who invents all sorts of distractions, purely material, which is the reason that one tires of things and is on the hunt for new distractions, all the while being distracted from the values of which one never tires, if only one is allowed to find them.

Often we see thoughts in the hearts of men that to appreciate perfection one must be acquainted with imperfection. You see we are concerned with all this, as it creates a hindrance for straight progress. We shall now present an example of a very simple nature, but one which frequently occurs and which proves the wrongness of the idea that bad is necessary for the appreciation of good.

Let us go out to an orchard, where fruit trees are plentiful and covered with fruit. You go to gather your harvest and you find among the fruit some rotten or misshaped ones. Will that make you appreciate the good fruit more or is it not rather felt as a hindrance in your work? Do you not say to yourself: 'bother all the rotten fruit, why cannot it all be good and why must we be hampered by having to assort instead of gathering the beautiful we receive by the love of God?'

You would never wish for bad fruit and so it is with everything. It is the evil still in you which gives you those ideas, as if you knew not of evil your souls would be purified.

We never said that God is not mercy [this answered to an interjection that mercy is one of the great virtues], but mercy in love, and if love comes to Him from His sinful children, love descends at once. That love, in truth, is in you and if you call for it, it unfolds itself in your very selves.

Forget evil...let the power of love govern you, then you can at once unite with God. Prevent such beliefs to exist on Earth that God knows and allows you to suffer. Shame on those who say such things and want evil to be found even in God. Do not let them soil the very name of the All Good by allowing waves of evil to play in words with you.

As told often in these messages, evil has no place in the world of eternal reality, the world of spirit, and, therefore, it is a passing illusion, a non-reality. To us, evil is a terrible "reality," but we must remember that it does not reach the actuality of the spirits' world.

Evil is not a part of our original nature or the nature of the physical world, as we shall soon see. But our observations that evil obstructs the advance of humanity toward good and sets limitations to our progress are obviously correct. Why is this so? We know that God is not aware of pain and sorrow; He only knows good. Therefore, pain and sorrow should be relegated to the realm of evil, being caused by influences not originating in the universe of love and light, which is God.

The contours of a vast drama start to emerge, enacted about us and in which we also take some part. A conscious, intentional activity opposes the advancement and perfection of life in all respects. We live among this unseen battle of opposing forces and are given free will to join the side of good, but we must be able to discern the invisible influences exerted by the corrupt enemy.

The stage is set for the more detailed messages to follow with this first exchange from the messengers on the personality and nature of evil.

Is evil an individual or a principle?

> *Evil is an inferior power, greatly helped by men.*

Do evil spirits exist?

> *Be sure of that.*

Is there an evil power?

> *Yes, the Bible informs you of that. You are the vessels through which God will conquer the spirit of evil.*

It is difficult to conceive of a devilish power, obstructing and limiting the power of God.

> *We cannot see God, but had a sight of the evil spirit or devil, as you call it. He has great power. God conquers and will defeat him through the work He set on us to free everything that is influenced by evil.*

Evil Regions

You said that you had a sight of the evil one. What was it like?

Everyone who lives on Earth has to pass through the region where evil dwells, but those clad in love and belief cannot be touched and just have a glimpse of what horror they escaped by nursing true love in their souls.

We have never told you that some spirits are not near you; on the contrary, the evil ones hover around you, or else we should not have the difficulties we have in bringing perfect harmony to you.

Do you imagine that the Earth is the real dwelling place of evil? No, Earth is created for souls who wish to better themselves. The place where evil has absolute power is the place nearest Earth.

Though evil dwells on Earth, the power of love and goodness dominates on the whole and is growing continually.

Evil's power is indeed great on Earth and so on the other regions nearest Earth. You heard that we in the highest regions do not want free will, but as you can now, with the continued illuminations you receive, understand, free will remains your self-inflicted possession, until you lose contact with evil and wish to be the humble servant, child, and friend of God.

Evil dwells in one respect much nearer Earth than any of the more purified spirits, and so its influence naturally comes easier in contact. Remember that it is the reason why the Bible talks of hell as being below. In reality, it means the sphere underneath us.

So often when men depart from Earth, as invariably all have to pass that region, if you watch carefully the one who is leaving the shell, you suddenly see a horror-stricken expression on his face.

Evil is still strong, though souls with elevated feelings after some years on Earth invariably feel the meaning of their being sent down, and they completely reject the thoughts of evil, and we assure you that evil burns in its own fire when seeing you becoming more and more seekers.

Have the low regions no rulers nor governance?

You ask about rulers in the lower regions? It resembles more life on Earth, but there is no ruler there either. On some parts there is real chaos, as everyone wants to do the same thing at the same moment. For those on the lower spheres, it is very difficult to see the thoughts of others and so they carry on similarly to on Earth, but yet it is different. On the lowest of all, evil has his spirits managing the followers of him. Little higher up spirits from higher spheres descend to give illumination about the perfect love and so it goes on progressing as they learn. If you on Earth could give up desires of ambition and live in pure love, you could feel the light of God a great deal stronger.

Evil Activities

Evil has waves but they do not radiate. Rays are living; they heal, give heat, etc., whereas, Evil waves are invisible and yet can be so strong that they penetrate through anything.

Evil waves are made of a different current to the good ones. Evil cannot exist next to goodness and love and withdraws his waves. Evil waves interfere with your pure waves and create confusion in your mind. Evil voices are slower than others.

Evil knows the thoughts of man. Evil possesses vast knowledge, but has no heart. Evil can influence forcibly.

Evil can create evil, which, however, has no life in the spirit world. Evil's creations have no souls, and so it is not life in the spirit sense.

Animals can be influenced by evil, who possesses a great knowledge from the life he had as a great messenger.

Evil is a great force and made animals venomous and fierce and gave fear to animals and men.

Evil can give life, but cannot create a soul. Part of our work is to counteract evil in nature.

Evil spreads disease and does, at the same time, wish man not to die. Evil is the opposite to progress, if you prefer this language, and manipulates the waves so as to cause illness. Evil poisons you with disease so that you in your sufferings should abuse God. Illness is evil and when sanitary conditions are modernized, he invents new diseases.

Our brain is inclined to be influenced by evil but the soul counteracts what the brain wrongly advises.

That brain—how much harm it has caused to mankind from its misuse and what a joyful scope for evil to play with. There are always evil spirits who wish to harm you around one, but if you listen carefully to your inner voices, you will soon discern the difference and darken them through your own trusting light. No true feeling is born from brain, but from within, and the brain is only a medium for the working out, not of emotions, but of problems.

Feelings like hatred are from the brain and could not come from within because what is from there is purely connected with spiritual existence. If we only listen to reason, the guardian's voice becomes dim and evil's influence increases.

The waves evil sends to Earth en masse stir up mistrust and doubts, and they touch nearly everyone, and so uneasiness enters the soul, creating disturbing thoughts.

Evil wishes invariably man to disbelieve in spirits, as evil knows too well that if man opens up to them and knows that he can be guided, faith and goodness would embrace Earth and evil be defeated. Evil is, therefore, anxious to urge man to believe that he can find an explanation to everything on Earth.

Evil created secretiveness concerning next life.

Evil is neither omnipotent nor omniscient and is the opposite to improvement and is destruction. Absolute destruction does not exist, whilst progress is in the love of God. Evil in his mischief often makes mistakes.

Evil gives the thought of doubt and the idea of getting out of life as much as you can, not knowing what happens to you after.

People hunt for new things—are ever on the outlook for excitement. There seemed to be a lot to satisfy their cravings and yet in their souls they have become more restless than ever. Now, can you imagine the Great One creating those ruthless cravings? No, as we told you, it is evil's doing. One of Earth's calamities is that one gets used to things and so continually wishes for something new. That feeling comes from evil's influence, who wishes for disturbances and restlessness in man.

Daily life is very fickle, and the more it follows evil, the stronger its unsteadiness. If this would not be the case, our waves of help could never fail.

Fear is one of evil's inventions, so any form of it is iniquitous. Fear must be replaced with wisdom and precautions instead. As long as the slightest fear exists, we put ourselves ready for evil's interference. This does not mean that we are deliberately giving chances to evil but the conditions on Earth are so constructed that as long as fear—an attribute unknown in the high spheres—exists, unwillingly harm can be done.

The waves of evil delight in playing with man whenever the question arises for a decision and you may get completely confused by the upsets of such tricks.

Evil is full of little tricks.

Any hesitation gives renewed opportunities to evil. If evil knows one is unsettled, he can damage you. Disorder creates chaos and invites evil work.

Evil is the greatest of cowards. If it knows you fear him not and knows his game, it will fear you and shun you. The mere thought of the high ones makes evil crouch in its darkness.

Fear is evil's greatest toy. Courage is defeat of evil, provided it is used wisely and knows where to stop. Balance and harmony are equally needed in courage, as in any other enterprise.

Any ugly thought is the making of evil.

Evil thoughts never travel on the straight road. Brooding is the influence of evil spirits.

Evil gives depressions.

Pessimism is the blood of evil. It leads to dissatisfaction and from that all evils have been born.

Evil nurses dissatisfaction and envy.

Evil makes his followers very fickle and variable. Goodness is calm, constant, and in perfect poise and balance.

Why should one live in a palace and the other have no hole to rest in? Believe us, it is all evil's doing and also caused by man's helplessness as to the management of their free will for their own benefit.

Evil, knowing that better conditions are most desirable and welcome by all of us, as it gives more chance to mankind for searching their inner selves, prevents by all kinds of little things such improvements.

Evil is so full of joy in putting up barriers, whenever it is possible. Evil teaches mankind to think highly of themselves.

The dogma of a subconscious self is invented by evil, which tries to make men believe that they can do all that the Great One does.

Evil's great aim is to wipe out from our hearts any individualism and idealism and make mere machines of us.

Evil wishes true artists to become mechanical.

Evil chiefly wants to influence man against love and gentleness and tries to make you deny God.

Love for beauty, love for animals, love for those who wish you ill, through that you can create a current which disturbs the evil.

Love crushes evil. Evil snarls at love.

Evil cannot bear joy, which has as its basis, true love. Evil tries to disturb [in nature] the perfect order which dwells in the Great One.

If evil would not interfere, the whole heavenly work of organising life on Earth would have been unnecessary, as body, or rather flesh, was only conceived to give a chance to those who left the guiding and Divine light.

Origins of Evil

Naturally, it is an incomprehensible mystery to us how a power of destruction could ever have issued from God's world of perfection. The mystery is heightened by the messages that evil is absolutely unknown in the highest spheres. From where, then, did evil come and how was it created in the first instance?

These questions are posed and will be answered by the messengers. The truth is that "God creates all, but all coming from Him is perfect and only changes when evil interferes," which leads to the quandary of how this intrusion occurs.

What will be the most difficult part in these messages to grasp is your statement that an individual evil power does exist.

> *Good friend, what you ask is not difficult for us to understand, but you need the spirit without flesh to grasp that. For mankind we think it incomprehensible, simply because on Earth, evil will himself make you disbelieve many of our statements.*

> *That God knows no evil, we told you repeatedly, and you either believe it or not. We cannot say more there. If mankind realises that the light in them is God, then, perhaps they will understand that they themselves can create to a certain extent and that having a free will, they, too, could invent, but, as the light of God cannot be looked at, that light itself could get a power just opposite to its glory. What we mean is that it is more likely that God combines both good and evil in that light which carries the corresponding opposite with itself, but if that is so, the love is so overpowering—as we certainly know for a fact—that God knows no evil, yet for one looking into that light longer than possible, it came to happen that that which is the opposite of love became the stronger in the messenger. These are all propositions of us spirits not so high as to know exactly what happened.*

> *The fact is that you cannot look into that light, and what we learn from studying is that it is not God, who has the evil, but it is the spirit, looking at it too long which creates that which is opposite to good and love and, as it is the result of looking into that light, the light must contain the opposite.*

> *Possibly it does not contain it at all, but is created by the spirit using the free will, not for advancing in good, but wanting to advance for his own sake.*

> *Now, remember that we said that probably His old messenger, though it need not be the oldest—he is eternal and evil is not—found that light too much for him, but not enough to make him God, as there is only one God. By that error evil was born. Errors occur continually, as spirits also have free will and that will does not always follow His light.*

Remember also that God made us each individual and machinery is non-existing here.

We would like to talk a little about punishment in a more effusive way. You may think that up here there is no punishment and that we can do only the right thing. That is true, generally speaking, but it may happen that a higher spirit does not quite follow the road he chose and the waves become entangled. Such a spirit immediately receives punishment, not deliberately, but as a natural and inevitable cause. He shadows the light and, thus, drops into a lower stage and the punishment is the greater for he knew what he did and that he must work his way [up] once more. Punishment is not given by God, but by yourself up here. Up here, it is all so pure that the merest hesitation creates shadows in the light, and when that happens, you must sink to a lower sphere.

Remember that on Earth when you send your linen to be washed clean and pure and when it is returned to you with a stain, you do not retain it, but return the same until it is free from stains. So must your soul remain, or else it falls back by itself to less light, until it can face purity.

You said that the light itself could get a power opposite to its glory and God, thus, carry evil in Him?

That was and is an assumption of ours. It matters little now how evil has started. The important thing is to wipe him out completely.

Remember that the higher the spirit dwells, the greater its knowledge, the more powerful—not in a commanding sense, but for inventing things— he is, so that it might very well have been born from himself. That again might have come from wanting to know too much. Supposing the Great One would also have the seed of evil in Him, that would be without His knowledge, as we know for certain that what is absolute good, love, and light cannot know of bad. But it could be different for those who are not God, yet possess a knowledge beyond human comprehension.

Even on Earth there have been born good souls who came down to help and then all of a sudden turned utterly bad.

We see from your thoughts that you are worried about certain points regarding the descending of spirits to Earth. Reflect and you will grasp and understand that there is no other alternative for those who turned away from the Great One, unless the spirit becomes evil altogether. Earth is by no means the worst for spirits, and they have every chance to purify themselves and return to God once more.

You must realise that absolute love and purity is such that the slightest sign of disharmony is enough for spirits to turn away from God, and such spirits cannot see light any more and begin to feel darkness around them. They feel lost among the pure, and so their wandering starts. So Earth was created for the settling down, and it gives a chance for reflection and purification. That they dread birth on or to Earth is very natural, though they are drawn to it as by a magnet.

You know by yourselves that there is pure beauty on Earth and that many souls dwelling on it are good people, and you cannot yourself find fault with them, but none of you is so pure as to understand what that absolute purity, that God is, means.

God made Earth to soothe your tormented souls. We say 'soothe,' but in reality He knows not that you are tormented. He knows that you turned away and, as he creates only good, Earth, if you take it as created, is good. This is almost impossible to explain as it is wholly a spiritual task. Let us now see whether we have come farther and are nearer to an explanation about how things, bad and good, advance.

We have told you previously and on several occasions that everything, even the Great One, is progressing: He in Himself and the others through events, experiences and mostly from His light. Now can you visualise a great spirit having suddenly a wish to look into the light of the Great One? This done—to you it seems a trifle, doesn't it?—well, once having done that, remember we serve and know not curiosity, the spirit was blinded, perhaps only for an earthly second, but that was enough for starting a journey away from God.

Now, we said that everything progresses and that spirit is also doing the same, but having turned from the light which blinded him, the progress will pronounce itself in bad things, so with time—as you say on Earth, but in ways as we say—it becomes evil and starts its new journey of damage. You see, little bad goes far ultimately, just as Christ says about God: 'little good goes far with my Father'. This means that if *you have started on the journey of goodness, great will your ultimate road be. This is nearer to the real truth than we [previously] have been able explain to you.*

Note: A few of the members had been discussing the earlier messages on evil in private and at the next sitting, the messengers offered their observations:

We anticipated a kind of confusion regarding some of our messages and particularly those on evil. It is almost impossible for us to represent in words what appears in our picture-waves, and if our statements seem obscure occasionally [to] you, we must be wise and either correct the messages or omit them, but we put a great importance on your conversation about evil because it is the dark spot mankind must wash into light. What we now realise stronger than ever is that evil is feared, yet one realises that that very fear is evil itself in every individual, speaking literally.

Do not get a contorted idea that to know of evil dooms you to destruction. This would be utterly against the influence our lectures desire to give to mankind.

We can say in true faith that not one soul on Earth is so pure that it can ignore the existence of that power we call evil. Your best and dearest friends have, even if only in thoughts, committed an offence towards what we now know is the Circle of perfect goodness, but it does not make them into bad people. Our idea of revealing to you evil even in the best is done for the purpose that everyone should in full force start or continue a campaign to teach tolerance, beauty, and continual work without the thought of what material benefit that work can bring to one.

The origin of evil, as we see it, was so minute but that for you continually witnessing horrors, it would not have been noticed; but as we also said, everything advances. That minute slip has become the growth of all that is bad. What we tell you to comfort you is that we know that evil will return to the light, and, therefore, we want to help you all to assist us to accelerate this blessing.

The wish of the high messenger to look too long into the light did not take place intentionally and you may say: how sad for the spirit to have done it.

But why should a longer gaze create the opposite to good, and why did the gaze ever take place?

Well on Earth you often get enthusiastic about beautiful things, about music, dancing, sport, and it happens, even if rarely, that you over-step your own capacity, and the good you had ends in crippling you or disabling you, etc. Why? Because your wisdom was miscalculated through your eagerness and free will.

Now the gaze had exactly the same result in a spiritual sense and was too much for the spirit, who gradually lost the balance of his wisdom, and his free will insisted on his becoming God himself. Such an idea can be created in one endowed with a certain amount of creative power.

It is not that the Great One has any evil in Him. No, we see more and more that that is not so, but for a spirit too much of the light means turning away from God, and if you turn from God and his light, you give birth to evil yourself. We all know that we must not gaze into God's light, but must be happy with the light He gives. This again is very hard to explain in words, and we do not seem to find a way to make you understand better, but perhaps by and by it will clear what we want you to grasp. We up here feel what we can do as far as the light of God is concerned and work accordingly. It is not that He forbids, but we must know how much we can stand.

Even you on Earth look into the fire, but would not step into it as you know you would be burnt. Yet it has happened that one could not control oneself and for example jumped into a burning crater and perished, though of course only in the flesh. We stop now.

You are all questioning continually about the origin of evil, which seems to occupy your mind far more than the origin of good. Do you know why? Because good has no origin. It is the very God Himself and, therefore, you do not question which also is the proof that all on Earth, at any rate nearly all, have some part of good in them, which is the spark of God, and what you know you have, you do not question about.

The problem of evil, on the other hand, constantly crops up in your minds and why? Because it is an alien condition, a growth that at first was very small and harmless, but what like everything else progressed and grew. Instead of growing in His light, it chose the way away from it and has become what it has become. It was such a small thing, a mere wish to glance longer than necessary. This might urge you to another question: why longer than necessary and how can that bring the ravaging of evil to such strength as it has brought itself?

The Great One is progressing the whole time in His own progress and that for eternity. To our minds, He always was and always will be, but we do not throw away the idea that through His circular progress, the waves did not embrace with the same intensity every [single] spirit. How could it when you know that God is not mechanical and that the one, who as we said, gazed too long into His light, missed the Circle, and gradually wished to become the Circle himself.

Remember you judge evil from an earthly point of view, but we talk of what happened much, much before the Earth was created. Evil started up here and not on Earth. Remember that Earth is the refuge for those who wish to get rid of evil, though his temptations follow you down.

From the previous messages, we should be able to draw some firm principles on the nature of evil and hopefully apply the knowledge to the betterment of our sojourn here on Earth.

In the first place, we learn that evil is an individual agency which grew from a transcendental act by a great spirit who longed to be equal to God. This statement was definite and does away with the argument that evil is attributable to other causes. It is interesting to realize that the senders of the messages are not able to give us fully authentic and complete reports concerning the actual birth of evil, but explain that they, with their deeper knowledge and proximity to the higher spheres, deduce what occurred. They emphasize, however, that exact certainty is unnecessary for our advancement and cannot be conveyed to human beings in an intelligible way. Their admitting of the limitations that they themselves have in this enigmatic subject should satisfy the reader as to the veracity of their statements on other subjects.

The conclusions we may draw from the messages would seem to be:

The Ultimate Being creates individual spirits out of love and for the sake of love, and in the absolute purity and innocence of His nature, He cannot conceive anything which is not love.

But love and individuality need a freedom of will and action—free devotion is the essence of love—and the spirits, created by God, were endowed with a free will. Through free devotion, expanding within the individual development of souls, love stays real and progresses. In wishing to perfect love, which is God Himself, and knowing, outside time, that His creation must be drawn by the light of love from which they sparkled out, God saw and sees His creation moving with Himself towards a heightened perfection which carries increasing bliss to all.

We, on the contrary, who know evil, may say that the free will implies the possibility of choice and that the created spirits were given a chance of moving away from the light and love of God—a possibility which God, in his innocence, was unable to entertain. From this possibility of drawing away, evil could develop in the long run, particularly as the spirits were given a certain inventive and creative power. That is what seems to have occurred.

In picturesque language, we are told that one of the great messengers of God, wishing to acquire more of His light than his state of progress allowed, found himself blinded by that error and, enveloped in shadows, reflexively withdrew from the light. This mistake is familiar to us on Earth, who, in a moment of poor judgment, motivated by greed or selfishness, have found ourselves in difficulty, unable to undo that which causes us grief and suffering. So it was that evil progressed, laying mistake upon mistake, always in a direction away from the love and light.

An individual being also must not transcend the orbit of activity which his own nature prescribes. That nature may, however, expand and develop progressively, and the orbit may widen immensely, but none can reach outside its scope until his nature becomes fully translucent to the strongest light of the Divine Source, which knows no limitation.

"As we live through thousands of dreams in our present life, so is our present life only one of many thousands of such lives which we enter from the other more real life… and then return after death. Our life is but one of the dreams of that more real life, and so it is endlessly, until the very last one, the very real life of God."

— Count Leo Tolstoy

11

REINCARNATION

The idea that human souls existed prior to their life in a perishable body is not novel, nor is the thought that souls, for their purification and advancement, must descend to Earth for this experience. In the messages that follow, we learn the truth of our purpose here on Earth. We learn that we have pre-existed and will continue our evolutionary paths from spiritual essence to perishable human form and back, as we rise higher or drift astray in our eternal quest to advance to the limitless perfection which is God's plan. Again, we learn that our free will decides the speed and success of this journey. The Creator needs His creation, which is part of Him for the progressive unfolding of His nature, and, thus, it becomes impossible for any soul to drift away forever. Our God-given choice is the factor which determines the duration of the cycle and the events which must be experienced until the light is finally reached.

Of course, many learned theologians and philosophers scoff at reincarnation. We will not go into all the arguments they advance, but one is common to their reasoning: the contention of memory loss.

This reasoning is as follows: No memory of an earlier life is preserved by human beings, and we lose all recollections of an existence on Earth when our brain dissolves. We cannot speak of a continued individual existence under such circumstances, as the memory, which is the registration that our ego contains of its own life, is shattered into parts

101

without any connecting link. Rebirth of a person without a memory of his previous life is equivalent to the annihilation of the person and the creation of a new being.

The spirit messengers refute the loss of memory argument with two explanations. The first one points out that we have to lose memory of prior incarnations when descending to Earth or earthly life would become strongly influenced through the recollections of earlier experiences. This would defeat the purpose of our free will, distorting the law of compensation for the sins and evil deeds of previous lives. Our spiritual purification can only take place in an unbiased state.

The second explanation is that we do not lose all memory of the key aspects of our existence. For example, many of us have experienced unexplained knowledge or familiarity with places or events during our present life. We may have a special talent or strong attraction to certain professions, interests, cultures, or geographical area. Someone may inexplicably yearn to visit Egypt or a village in England, although there is no clear reason the desire persists. We may learn a foreign language with little effort, complex mathematics or scientific study may come to us instinctively. Prodigies become accomplished musicians or mathematicians at an early age. A young man or woman excels in a sport from the first attempt—they are "naturals." These leanings, preferences, skills, and talents are memories; they are traits that were strongly present or developing in a previous life. Our personalities survive our mortal existence; they are immortal.

Besides, who of us can now recall all the events of our present life? Unless a compelling emotional impact punctuated the event, most of our memories of ten, twenty, or thirty years ago are buried far from conscious recall. Why should our inability to remember details of a life hundreds of years in the past reject that life any more than our lack of recollection of many portions of this life deny our present existence?

In any event, we are told that a record of our previous lives' constructive events is kept in picture form in the world of reality and that, though we are prohibited from seeing it now, we will view a history of all our Earthly activities and regain lost knowledge of pre-existence. Our spirit teachers will use this "film" of our lives to point to the areas in need of improvement to aid in the progression of our souls. It is one of the illusionary effects of Earthly life that we are isolated and separate from the whole of creation of which we are a part.

Now the messengers speak of birth and death.

It is perhaps hard to believe that God needs souls on Earth or rather spirits [in the world of reality], and it is perhaps futile to try to explain a thing which has no explanation and must be accepted as truth and fact just like you accept the sun, the stars, etc. You try to explain why they are there, yet it does not help to make you better. Let it remain a mystery, but never believe that God made any mystery. Now if you accept this, as we accepted it long ago, you will find it easier to grasp that we can also be of use to Him. That light in each individual, given by Him, can never be extinguished, and it is that light which will ultimately make all souls and spirits return to Him.

If, therefore, knowing that you have something of God in you, you go on developing it, correcting your faults, rejecting the tempting voices of evil, and work many hours a day to improve your talents and capacities, you will know that you are in a way helping the Great One. He has given you the free will to enable you to choose and decide for yourselves. If you beautify a flower and make it look better, you are helping God, and so with everything and through you, His perfection is perfecting itself. It is different with the angels, who have never turned from Him. They never asked, but they just followed.

We are from the light of the Great One and, therefore, He needs us, but we drifted from Him and we now work to gather all back.

Are predestination and free will co-existent?

Predestination and free will are co-existent. The whole mystery of the humans is based on that. They are both true. Your coming to Earth is a sort of penitence. If you study yourself, you will discover in time that all sorts of impressions originate from your spirit life, which, for reasons we shall not tell you, you had to leave to come and pay for sins on Earth.

The great values you acquired before you descended to Earth, you find awaiting you on your return here, provided you are purified enough to see those values, which are all in pictures; you can acquire them again if you feel that you are ready for them.

A soul may sink from a higher existence to a lower. Every new-born is given a chance for high development. Those who sink lower according to the law of spirits and as a natural cause are obliged to go through a more severe test than that in Earth's purgatory.

You know that to descend to Earth is a punishment inflicted by yourselves on yourselves and a recollection of the reason for that punishment would make unnecessary the gift of free will and also take away all credit for your improvement.

Do not forget that you were a pure spirit and given a great part of God's light and wisdom. Although you have thrown away that part of glory, you could not throw off the part which is God in you, and so it is no wonder that moments occur when the spark of your past existence flashes out and gives life to someone new.

What value has immortality if we do not remember the past?

Good friends, you do not remember everything during your life on Earth and why should you? Yet, you do not deny that you are alive. So much in earthly life is not worth remembering, and were you to remember the existence before you descended, progress would not be of the same value or significance. The fact that one discusses the possibility of all this ought to be a definite proof of life before and after. Nothing which is discussed by man is coming from purely Earth-bound imagination. It all originates from the past, however dim the recollections are. The sole object of life on Earth comes from the life of the spirit.

You cannot—can you?—admit that either nature or God could be so senseless as to destroy what it has created. We know that you would like to know all we now see, but that you shall not do on Earth, as otherwise you would not be able to clean yourselves for the sake of cleanliness. Ultimately, you do recollect all worthy of recollection and so will, thus, learn how you progressed.

Do we not lose memory altogether?

Correct. Besides not one of you on Earth is without a faint recollection of some past or other. That little in each of you works deeper than you realise. You are all so matter of fact, wanting to lay your hands on solid ground, either not wishing or lacking the trust that something deeper than the intellect is guiding you along the path which is either your purification or your farther prison in the hereafter.

Descent

Visualise a horizontal line vibrating in divine light, freely drifting along in happiness and progress. Suddenly, it is drawn by an opposite magnet; this of course is not strong enough to oppose the interfering element. It immediately becomes dark and the vibrations change. This is when it is born to Earth. But it still goes on vibrating, and if love dominates all bad attributes, it gradually regains its light and true vibrations. You can see yourselves the light or darkness, whatever it may be, changing in the expression of the soul. That which vibrated, the line, speaking in an allegory, continues the same as before without any change of its origin, except that it gains more and more light as it advances or darkens farther and is drawn, not towards Earth, which is rightly called one of the cleaning stations, but towards the bad altogether, though that bad is an illusion to us who know that only good is truth.

Most of the spirits have several possibilities, which they see before entering flesh, and during the period on Earth their inner voice guides them to the right way, but their free will, disturbed by evil, does not always follow. How the possibilities are decided belongs to the final spheres to know.

Are the pictures which we see before our descent to Earth, representing our future existence, the outcome of a decision by God?

God does not know of evil, so He cannot decide your fate. That is your doing. Each spirit that has sinned sees its life up here, and what it will have the instant it has sinned, as to think of oneself, to see oneself, is one of the greatest punishments. Again, [it is] brought upon one by oneself.

You are allowed to enter the body that will suit best for your inclinations. You are also advised whilst still a spirit which body would be best for your development. Evil, though, can make you believe that the wrong body is suitable, when he knows it will bring disaster to your spirit which is sent to Earth for purification.

The spirit enters the body the moment the embryo begins to move. Can you imagine a greater punishment for a spirit, who lived free, never knowing tiredness, hearing, seeing divine things, having the knowledge of eternal light, though not having seen it, then suddenly to be put into a living armour that controls mind and is jamming all the actions of the spirit and needs constant rest and care and prevents on every road the actions without interruption. Spirits are afraid of birth as you are of death.

How are spiritual qualities inherited from earthly parents?

You do not inherit habits or characteristics. Spirits, who enter bodies are destined to be born in such constitutions of flesh, nerves, etc., which will suit the development of their personalities, but nothing is inherited as you will assume on Earth. Some undeveloped souls simply copy others and take up their habits, especially bad ones like drink, lies, stealing and others because evil is standing nearby, and they are too weak to resist temptations, but we emphasise to you all that every spirit is individual, regardless of parents hence in so many cases false family ties.

"There are only two ways to live your life. One is as though nothing is a miracle. The other is as though everything is a miracle."

— Albert Einstein

12

REGISTRATION OF EARTHLY LIFE

We now see that an eternal bond exists between the soul on Earth and its former life as a spirit; that what psychologists find as our subconscious mind is our spirit self, faithfully and continuously orchestrating the infinite "heavenly mathematics" responsible for the biological miracle we call our mind and body. Next, we learn that a stream of information continually flows between the two worlds, automatically registering our constructive thoughts, which vibrate, creating images representing the state of the individual soul while on Earth. The images are permanent and are reviewed by us and our spirit advisers each time we return to their domain. We are expected to learn from the record of our earthly phase and progress to higher levels. Of course, we can choose to ignore the lessons and turn away from the light, delaying our eventual ascent.

Up here, we register every thought of earthly people if the thoughts are constructive in a sense that makes a difference to their own life or influences through their waves the lives of others.

Only those which are felt and through them active decisions result are registered.

From the pictures in your spirit life, you shall read your earthly actions and see the right or wrong you did in life. Only constructive thoughts and memories matter.

Every individual has his own special record and in different grades so that it cannot be mistaken, each according to its past standard flooded by light. The pictures are representing your whole existence of the past and that is what you leave behind. But if you would recollect those pictures, which, by the way, you sometimes do see in your sleep, you would know all that will happen to you. Of course, we do not include minor events. Were you to remember those pictures, there would be no merit in your improvement. We can see your future from your past pictures and you on Earth with your thought [pictures] help us to see farther as you progress or decline.

Every soul has the outline of their life in pictures. Your actions fill up the space inside.

Are the pictures from our life on Earth automatically recorded, or is it done by high spirits?

This is almost impossible to explain in such a manner as to make you see clearly.

Up here, we have substances and wave vibrations which when reaching to a certain point become colours. Why? Because, as we said, colours are living or, better said, colour is life. So now what left Earth is to you invisible, and you say it is dead. Quite the contrary. When it leaves you, we mean thoughts, etc., and comes to the sphere of the spirits, it takes up, or rather, becomes the colour of its master, and, thus, we recognise the owner of the thoughts and other things. How could you otherwise imagine you could be recognised?

The colours represent your spirit when here and your soul's condition when still on Earth. They vary in brightness, shades, etc., according to your nature. Some are dull, some are quite clear but not too brilliant, some, as we said, dazzling. They have a multitude of variations. These thought-waves, after reaching the world of the spirits are carefully arranged each to its section, where they continue to vibrate. Thus the pictures never change and present an eternal reading and also an eternal lesson.

You said that colour is living?

As you know, persons have colour around them which is called on Earth the aura. Well, every individual has that aura in various shades and that really represents the soul of the individual. A flower has colours, and the colours represent their life so that in their case colour is also living. You can never get accurately the colour of a living kind into a colour manufactured. Colour has magnetism and electric vibrations, therefore in man's aura, the colors change continually if you take the trouble of making a careful observation. Colors depend greatly on the speed of the circular waves that vibrate them. We cannot at present explain it clearer as this—to you a phenomenon—belongs to spirit life where it seems so natural and simple.

The pictures represent the acts of your life on Earth, and so the calculations out of it show the pictures of what you will become, what they will receive, according to your love and progress. Your chief events are all known before you descend to Earth, but you forget them, as you must, and your free will and inner voice guides you and tells you what to do, and if you do not listen to that, certain pictures will change, as you then once more listen to evil voices. Unless you work with a balance of mind, the pictures will be all muddled up.

Can the main things on the picture disappear?

Nothing of a constructive nature is lost on the pictures and we up here only see the pictures of the good spirits or souls.

"The measure of a life, after all, is not its duration, but its donation."

— Corrie ten Boom

13

LIFE'S DURATION

The duration of our earthly life is decided by God, but is not measured in terms of a mechanical time, which has no meaning in the world of reality. We receive deliverance when the picture of our life coincides with the pictures set for the ending of our stay on Earth. The duration is defined in terms of result and in such a way that everyone, relatively speaking, gets the same chance and opportunity as other fellow wanderers on Earth of becoming purified to the extent expected from Him. Free will obviously plays an important part in completion of the expectations set by God.

There is a big problem we should like to explain to you somehow, yet we wonder whether it is possible to make you understand what we mean. It is concerning the fixed hour of departure of the soul from Earth.

The way we told it to you is really too simple. Whilst in reality for you, who have a regular fixed time—daily, monthly, yearly—everything is regulated according to those calculations, it is not so with us up here, where time is perpetual and is not a regulated concern. Now, even on Earth, you cannot regulate death, even though your hours and minutes are regulated. The physician, who often sits by the bedside of the dying, how wrong he is in declaring the length of the life of the dying. Sometimes he errs by as much as two or three weeks. This perhaps will give you a little picture of the fact that there is no time even on Earth; as soon as life's duration faces calculations of time, it fails to succeed.

Now up here, where the life of souls on Earth is decided by the Great One, it has nothing to do with time, but depends on certain waves and lights which, regardless of time, reach the soul on Earth when God has decided. Now you will perhaps be able to see a fraction farther how things are standing up here. That which is is perpetual and, therefore, it is so difficult to put it into arrangements of weeks and months. In one respect, we have trouble to see death at all, because the soul never dies and always shines before us regardless of body.

Is malady not responsible for death?

Death is independent of malady, as God knows no such thing as malady. At the same time, evil gives illness, when he thinks death is not far. His calculations are not infallible, and the free will can also prolong or shorten. On Earth, everything is in time and here everything is outside time, having no end and no beginning. This is something you will never really grasp whilst on Earth, so never try to do so, but accept it.

Statistics show that improved sanitary conditions prolong life and that the death rate has steadily gone down. How does this tally with your statement?

We like your exactitude—the only route for wisdom and clarity of matters. We understand fully the importance you attach to life's duration on Earth and that you wish to receive more clear explanation. You say life is prolonged by improved sanitary conditions, by better water supplies and by a great many other advanced arrangements. We do not contradict the fact that it is so. That sanitary conditions are advancing is only to our delight and influences.

Dirt is evil's delight, and cleanliness the taste of heaven's purity. To you, it seems that life is prolonged by these improvements, yet it is only relatively so, or else the cleanest in the past and present would unconditionally live to be old, and you know best that that is not the case. You do not know that God's decision is not like that of man, but is varied in a million ways. You could not know what passes through earthly thoughts in men which creates such waves for the Great One to detach the spirit from the body.

We never said–have we?–that we know why God stops the spirit continuing in the body, but we always said that when He decides for man to die, he dies. Death of man is not from disease which could be scientifically proved if only trouble is taken. We repeat one thing: the key of heavenly mathematics only belongs to God, as He is that heavenly key Himself.

Please explain more fully the original question concerning illness and death.

We repeat: illness cannot separate your spirit from the flesh, as that is the decision of God. At the same time, it must be said that in your view it seems so, as the two are so closely connected if you are nearing the time of your voyage.

Evil, in most cases, poisons you with disease for two reasons: the one that he hopes that you in your suffering will abuse God once more, and the other because he delights in agony and pain. You may well have read that in the past many a famous man took delight in watching his neighbour being tortured and revelled in it wholly.

That illness is not the cause of death is proved by many who, bodily worn out and finished, skin and bone, have from one second to another regained strength and health of the organs. That is and was when God's decision was miscalculated by evil, and we spirits succeeded to restore flesh to its normal function by an influx of pure waves to the sufferer whose deliverance had not yet come.

How can you reconcile the statement that evil produces great disasters but God alone decides the hour of death?

Yes, we realise the difficulty you have in understanding such happenings, but do not forget that evil is on constant watch over mankind and is the only power which continually makes mistakes, whilst the Great One cannot err. Why, you ask? For the simple reason that purity cannot err as erring is bound to be, somehow or other, opposed to good, hence belonging to evil.

Now when evil inflicts a great disaster or calamity, he is most often playing into the waves of the Great One, because, say for instance, a train wreck, the people perishing were sent to that train specially as their second for

Earth departure had arrived. So evil did not do the harm you believed, except in a material loss. For you, of course, it is hard to grasp that it is all to the good to leave Earth, but for the soul it is the rebirth into its real home.

Evil can prevent departure by cunning manipulations of the waves. It does not succeed for good, but creates disturbances; also, there are many other things done by him which you could not possibly understand on Earth. You can only grasp facts and that which you have seen, heard, or touched. You can build in your imagination on that, but the subtle, invisible work of the wave-system cannot yet be understood by mankind.

No one on Earth has the right to take his life or the life of others. Criminals must be punished as to leave them loose is a danger to mankind, but to dispose of their lives is no man's business. This sort of death makes great confusion here, as we know that their penitence has not ended. Thus, the executed soul is immediately re-entering a new body, and the struggle with evil begins again. So you see that when you believed you got rid of a criminal, you made a new one instead. It is far better to put the fellow under lock and careful watch. Go to him with a loving heart, open up the possibilities and chance—just as for all others—he has. If they try to see the truth, they shall do so and they are then given the opportunity of bettering themselves and repent for their sins.

God is the symbol of mercy, and a little goodness goes far with Him and He is the symbol of tolerance also because He knows not of intolerance. Verily we tell you, God cannot yet be grasped by man, who made Him after his image, when the only resemblance man has of Him is unseen to man.

"John Quincy Adams is well but the house in which he lives at the present time is becoming dilapidated. It's tottering on its foundations. Time and the seasons have nearly destroyed it. Its roof is pretty well worn out. Its walls are much shattered and tremble with every wind. I think John Quincy Adams will have to move out of it soon. But he himself is quite well, quite well."

— John Quincy Adams

14

DEATH AND AWAKENING

Why are people afraid of dying? This is a very complicated affair for the messengers to explain. First, everyone—to varying degrees—dreads the unknown. That fear, as all others, is the creation of evil. Secondly, if we had complete trust, we would know that what dies never really lived except to allow the soul to perform on Earth. What really lives cannot die. This may seem incomprehensible, but it is so, and to the messengers it is clear.

On Earth, death gives the impression of everything coming to an end. This sad impression has been imposed or influenced by evil. Souls invariably have a part of the Great One in them and, as we said, that never dies. There is no death, but only a re-birth of the soul to its real sphere.

There are special magnetic waves holding body and soul together. If the soul is ready to leave the body, these waves detach themselves and free the soul from its prison. How that happens we do not quite know. All we can say is that a sudden detachment of the soul from the body is rather a shock to the spirit.

The severing of the spirit from the flesh cannot be done but by the Great One. At the same time, events must fit a circle corresponding to such states which necessitate the departure of the spirit. This may happen in a second and may also be delayed. Evil has not real power in keeping

119

a soul alive, but can create conditions which necessitate a prolongation, and that ought not to be difficult to understand; it explains why so often, and in so many cases, delays occur.

We would like you to think a little about the fact that the blood in your body is manipulated by waves. When the spirit leaves the body, the blood stops running and coagulates. Were it not so, you could by extra heat start the blood to flow again and so restore life, but that is absolutely impossible. Why? Because the body can only function through the spirit encased in it. The spirit, however, is much more elastic than the body. It is only attached by that, to you, invisible substance which the Great One detaches from you when you are ready to meet the circle which determines to start a new existence in the world of the spirits.

It is not so, as you imagine that you die and your new place is ready waiting for you. Not at all. Each soul leaving the body must have a place to which they will fit in, and order must exist, an order of a heavenly nature, which is different to order on Earth. The life of man is mathematically calculated. It has to fit in with actions, waves, etc., stars, communities, elements and man's own free will. This all happens outside time yet must coincide with the laws born from the Great One.

You must realise that there is an enormous difference when flesh, nerves, etc., are left behind, and that the values change greatly, though at first the change is not complete and the spirit not completely free from the sensations it left behind and it may even occur that you believe you desire all things you desired on Earth, but those desires are soon vanishing and you then understand the freedom of the soul. A prisoner, long enough in chains, cannot at once realise his freedom and almost mechanically continues his routine from prison life, but that goes also with time.

At first you do not realise that you are over. It is like a heavy sleep when you do not know where you are. But after a while, reality becomes clearer, and the happiness of the bodiless freedom is unbelievable.

When one joins the world of the spirits, at first one is still clear in the recollections of Earth; in fact, most spirits arriving here are half on Earth. After a while they start developing, but are unable for a period to talk to souls on Earth, though in many cases they are anxious to let you know they are contented and happy.

It is so natural to feel sorrow at a friend's departure. One grieves for oneself even if one's belief is absolute. For us who see souls on Earth as well as the spirit, it is not possible to have unhappy feelings, but for you it is natural, though it does not help the departed.

If one can get that feeling of aloofness and feel the soul departed, of course one lives in quiet happiness and brings conditions on Earth which are helpful.

Imagine a person going to a place where he or she is unable to write, though communications from those left behind reach him or her; supposing those communications are full of lamentations and longings for the person, how grieved he or she must become, not being able to report that only happiness and good things are around him or her, whilst if cheerful conditions are contained in all letters received, calm and peace will surround the absent.

Look up and rejoice for those who are allowed to shorten their earthly time.

Death is the greatest promotion.

Those who trust in the true life which awaits all ought to rejoice for their friends being called up and only be sorried for their own selves having to part for a time. Would you not prefer having the blue sky under your heads instead of being urged into fog? The first is the state of our lives, and the second is the condition of earthly beings. Is it to be wondered at that we long to make you realise that only those who are left behind are the ones to be pitied as they remain in darkness and uncertainty as to the life up here and that we are trying all we can to show you that God's light and not the sun's is happiness everlasting. Do you understand our fervent wish to crush that which brought spirits into life on Earth?

Nothing exposes the difference between our world of illusion and the world of reality more clearly than the concepts of birth and death.

While we celebrate the arrival of a new-born child and the beginning of new life, the event inspires no elation in the spirit world. In the heavenly spheres, the birth of the baby on Earth means a "death" of a spirit entity. That birth coincides with the descent of a spirit from real life and entails the pain of becoming enveloped in an armor of flesh after experiencing the incredible lightness and freedom of a spirit.

Nothing typifies the difference in our two realities than the manner in which mortals and spirits differ in their reaction to birth and death. To them, our death is rebirth and an event to acclaim with joy, yet we grieve and mourn the "loss" of someone dear to us.

As for possessive, proud parenthood, we learn that the child chose us, and we are but caretakers and guardians for a short period of time while the human fulfills his or her heavenly assignment.

We look at the body and treat it as the essence of the departed, preserving it with chemicals and commenting on how good a job the undertaker performed on the corpse, as if the casket held the life we loved.

Meanwhile, the soul who discarded the body we grieve is overjoyed with its freedom from physical imprisonment, the confines of gravity, the burden of time, and the truth-inhibiting limitations of a human brain.

The two big events of earthly existence look strangely different as seen within the frame of life in this low region, compared to the reaction of those in the timeless and euphoric spheres where the departure of friends to Earth is viewed with concern and their return hailed with relief and delight.

We must make up our minds and decide which view harmonizes with the inner sense of reality within us. Those who have traveled temporarily to the other side during a near death experience agree with the messengers' description of death, and many were reluctant to return to this existence.

May we eventually attain an attitude reflected in a sermon given by Henry Scott-Holland (1847-1918), Canon of St. Paul's Cathedral, while the body of King Edward VII was lying at state at Westminster:

Death is nothing at all.
It does not count.
I have only slipped away into the next room.
Nothing has happened.

Everything remains exactly as it was.
I am I and you are you, and the old life that we lived so fondly
together is untouched, unchanged.
Whatever we were to each other, that we are still.

Call me by my old familiar name.
Speak to me in the easy way which you always used.
Put no difference in your tone.
Wear no forced air of solemnity or sorrow.

Laugh as we always laughed at the little jokes we enjoyed together.
Play, smile, think of me, pray for me.
Let my name be ever the household word that it always was.
Let it be spoken without effort, without the ghost of a shadow
upon it.

Life means all that it ever meant.
It is the same that it ever was.
There is absolutely unbroken continuity.
What is death but a negligible accident?

Why should I be out of mind because I am out of sight?
I am but waiting for you, for an interval, somewhere very near,
just around the corner.

All is well.
Nothing is hurt; nothing is lost.
One brief moment and all will be as it was before.
How we shall laugh at the trouble of parting when we meet again!

"Lord, make me an instrument of thy peace.
Where there is hatred, let me sow love,
Where there is injury, pardon;
Where there is doubt, faith;
Where there is despair, hope;
Where there is darkness, light;
And where there is sadness, joy.

O Divine Master, grant that I may not so much seek
to be consoled as to console,
to be understood as to understand,
to be loved, as to love.

For it is in giving that we receive,
It is in pardoning that we are pardoned,
and it is in dying that we are born to eternal life."

— Francis of Assisi

15

TEACHINGS FOR DAILY LIFE

The next series of messages deals with how best to conduct our lives on Earth in order to insure the optimum foundation for our transition into the world of reality—the spiritual world. The messengers are sharing their perceptions, thoughts, and observations of human characteristics and conduct that are deemed important to the quality of spiritual advancement. They inform us, again, that our predominant personality, thoughts, and attitudes are carried with us into the heavenly realms and determine the level we enter into the hereafter. Humans can, if they so desire, conduct themselves on Earth in such a manner as to bypass the lower regions of Earthbound souls who are not aware of their divine heritage and destiny.

The lower regions are not pleasant and represent the traditional concept of purgatory. In his book, *Excursions to the Spirit World*, Frederick Sculthorp—an accomplished astral traveler—describes visits to the regions populated by Earth-bound souls whose unawareness of their divinity fated them to continue after death as they had in earthly life. Some of them even got up every morning, packed a lunch, and went to work at a job they had despised in life. These souls eventually ascend to the higher levels, but progress is slow and they are doomed to return many times to earthly incarnations.

Our messengers do not want man to suffer and stagnate in the lower spheres. Since we carry our predominant beliefs and personalities with us to the heavenly existence, it is possible and highly preferable to develop as much consciousness and spiritual literacy while here and enter God's kingdom as many tiers above the earthly plane as we can merit. It should be clear to the reader by now that this is the main purpose of the messages—to help us advance as quickly as we are willing to the regions of the high souls. It is only from those lofty planes that we exude waves powerful enough to join them in their struggle against humanity's ignorance and evil's consequent destructive power over Earth's populace.

When reading these lessons, you may feel that, although the messages are timeless, some of the instructions in this section seem to address old-fashioned lifestyles. That is because of the era during which they were given. But it is easy to mentally adjust the admonitions to apply to life today.

Conscience

You often talk about your conscience. You know that it is non-existent in the sense you believe. Trust that it is our voices which create that sensibility. In the essence of your being, you are all good, as the Great One could not create evil.

Your soul resembles the sun that shoots out multi-coloured rays. The rays vary in strength and size but remain all the same, the sun. At times it is covered by clouds interfering with its warmth and healing power, sometimes even enveloped in almost complete darkness, but remember the sun is still underneath it all intact and pure. So it is with the soul.

Evil is the cloud, but the day is not so far off when those clouds will be dispersed for eternity, and His light will shine through all and everything. The conscience is the good in man which received the good spirit influences.

The instant you are aware of your faults, you are on the mend. It is for those who never study their thoughts, being unaware of their errings, that life up here will be very difficult.

A resolution to become better is a guiding wave and opens up grounds into which it becomes easy for us to pour in wisdom, light, and pure knowledge. You also gather and draw new and pure and noble souls around you and towards you by such a decision.

Much thinking in peace and quiet makes you deeper. Relaxation is vital if you wish to work hard and well. One can almost, so to speak, step out of the body when in a relaxed state and achieve truly great things. Hardly anyone is capable on Earth continually of remaining relaxed, as that would mean no fatigue, and evil sees to that, we tell you. Relaxation ought to become one of man's mottoes. It is the herald of purification as a relaxed soul could never err, as then they or it could not fail to recognise the guiding voices of the spirit world.

The most powerful way to hear the guiding (or rather the continual) inflow of the spirit waves is to close the functioning of the brain and to make that instrument silent. It is not difficult, except when your brain says so. Your soul knows so much more than your brain, yet your brain makes its activity dead.

Doubt

Let us understand the tragedy of doubt, and let us see how to correct it. That you doubt your fellow men is less to be wondered at knowing, or at least feeling, in a remote way, that it is through a fellow spirit, sunken away from God, that you had to descend into the wretchedness of life.

That you doubt God follows as a matter of ignorance, yet we know for certain that there is not one soul on Earth who—however deep it is hidden in them—is not aware of the existence of God and that is why, comparatively, you are all forgiven your sins, as the way that hidden feeling is developed in you so you bring yourselves closer to Him, Who never takes but is ever giving.

Now we come to the part of doubt in oneself, the most difficult of all doubts, as there you are left to yourself and no one—not even God—can help you. We up here abhor from that terrible misery.

When you think that you have a soul embodied in flesh which rots away after you have freed yourself from your exile—yes and you have that soul continually watered by the higher spirits, unceasingly fed by divine inspiration, yet you doubt, for example, that you can help a person in distress and you do nothing. This applies to innumerable other things also.

You doubt your own belief in God and so try to destroy that ever existing, even though remote, feeling of God's power. In one word: by doubting your capacities, you deny God and give farther scope for evil's playing with you.

Away and down with doubt. Know that you have a right to present your opinions to the world, even if it may seem droll to your neighbour. If you trust in yourself, you admit God in you, and so you allow your soul to progress. Doubt is an alliance to defeat. Your own free will is the weapon to win over evil.

Progress is the outcry of all of us, but progress without the slightest doubt of a possible standstill or obstacles. That is entirely eliminated, hence our glorious knowledge that every wave brings us nearer the whole. This is the attitude for earthly souls if they want their yearnings fulfilled.

It is a strange characteristic of mankind that they put obstacles of doubt for events to happen which they long for most. All through the ages, this has been the case and is still happening. Is it the work of evil, or is it the result of not always feeling the light of God?

Why doubts always? If you only could enjoy 'today' without asking continually what 'tomorrow' will bring? We tell you that neither 'today' nor 'tomorrow' can thus be enjoyed. Live in love and light 'today', the 'morrow' shall bring its delight also. Keep to this, and you shall live in peace.

Every little doubt defers the waves of trust, and so it becomes impossible to reach high up. The hardest thing on Earth is to have an unbiased trust.

God cannot be questioned, but has to be understood within you. Where is true belief when one demands proof? No proofs can be real proofs to those who doubt—and who believe and trust have the proofs within them. Sometimes we would like you to become more a child. Only the best can come to those who may become children at times. If you watch nature, it nearly always presents a cheerful spectacle because nature is the least spoilt by evil.

Individuality

Mankind has one ambition and that is to look the same as their fellow man. Do not men and women realise that they, each of them, are individual beings and that which suits one, does not suit the other? In fact, by wishing to copy the other, they kill that which is the real thing in themselves, and those will arrive up here lost and alone.

It is not necessary to have the same views, as long as belief is there and opposed to the ills of evil. Man is individual, which gives to your (as well as our world) such a variety. The beauty of the pure individual spirits consists of their directing their main gift towards God.

We are definitely against collective knowledge won through the exploring of others. It is false in its essence and it deliberately destroys your individuality, which is one of God's greatest creations. If that individuality instead was allowed to grow in yourself, the greatest part of the troubles amongst men would gradually die out.

You must use your own individuality and not borrow from others. That lowers you. We try to make you independent and free from the influence of your fellow-man. This is most essential. If you do not trust your own judgment, your own feelings and emotions, you become a nonentity and that darkens the light which tries to shine through you.

Go always by your intuition, and cast away the advice of others. Few, very few, are impartial on Earth and generally their advice is closely connected with their own interests. Only abstract conversations are of value and of use for the development of one's own soul.

Selfishness

Beware of being selfish and always think of others before you think of yourself; a much greater joy will then enter your heart and soul. The true secret of glory lies in nursing your neighbour before you nurse yourself.

Selflessness is true godliness.

Forget your own importance which, though quite mighty, is very small once you get here.

Those who sit at home continually praying for the salvation of their souls, souls filled with selfishness, will have a very hard time up here where exclusiveness is non-existent. We admit to no egotism, nor those possessed with envy or malice, nor jealousy, because they are the attributes to self-love, *taught by evil. A thief is less bad than the former ones. It is those sins which ruin and create waves which destroy beauty and goodness.*

What creates trouble on Earth is that you are living in constant dissatisfaction because you give the greater part of your thoughts not for your development, but to the wish of [outdoing] your neighbour.

If you on Earth could give up your desires of ambition and live in pure love, you could feel the light of God a great deal stronger. Ambitions take such a part of your lives and think of their futility. Even if through ambition you reach to the highest on Earth, what are you bringing to us? Nothing, we say, unless what is concentrated around God and His love. For that, though, you need not have ambition, as it is in your hearts you find that illumination and no outside influence can take you there.

How lonely those spirits will feel whose only aim in life was to seek for the admiration of others. We do not say: neglect your daily work, but in whatever you do, keep love first in your heart, and if you attain success in life materially, be humble about, remembering that here you will not be treated with greater respect than your subordinate, provided of course that both allowed love to rule before anything. You ought to live—all of you—in the reality of love's truth and be ready to give up every possession, were you asked to do so. That is the only way if you are hoping for the light of God and happiness in defeating evil.

Possessions

Possessions are vastly overrated, as property seldom has given anyone a vision of love. In fact, possessions often destroy love, and if you lack love, whether you are wealthy or poor, you cannot be happy.

Souls who love possessions, but are not dependent on them, are what we call seekers, as they find the real emotion in the spiritual and not in the material things. You cannot be a seeker if you are unwilling to part with your property, as when you leave flesh, you will still long for it and everything connected with it.

The Great One's greatest messenger, Christ, never said that you must not possess riches or houses or beautiful things. What He said was that you must love and trust God before thinking of your possessions, and if it needs to be so, give it all. Love is the only thing you carry with you to eternity.

Power of possessions is the killing of faith and spiritual advancement. The majority of men on Earth believe that property is happiness. It is lack of observation that makes this belief so universal. The real treasures are in your soul.

Possessions are nothing as long as you do not attach any importance to them. If you do not mind parting with earthly treasures, you can keep them. The difficulty lies with those who are dependent on possessions.

What people must learn is to search their inner self. After some time they will find what no material possessions can give. But we agree that all men ought to have enough to live upon as otherwise their bodies get too weak for the understanding of what passes within them.

Do not care for money. Lies can be bought with it. Do not fancy yourselves better than others. Arrogancy is a great sin. Your soul counts and not your position.

If you are continually tormenting yourself, always thinking how this or that may affect your own personality, you are training your soul to copy the pattern of evil and the condition you nurse will follow you to the hereafter, and, thus, you will live in torment and displeasure.

The poorest man on Earth may be the nearest to the highest up here if during flesh existence he carried pictures of happiness in himself and led a life of internal love and light. This is easy to understand as nothing of value in the sense of material things and nothing that perishes can or does follow your soul when leaving Earth.

It is only natural that your life up here is and will be continued by or in the feelings and thoughts you possessed on Earth.

Charity

It is not so much the actual gift as the very thought of others that elevates you to the light of God. All great things' source rests in the welfare of your neighbour.

Be generous, not only in giving, but in thinking charitably towards your neighbour, provided of course, that your neighbour is worthy of thoughts.

Unless one does an act absolutely spontaneously without hoping for favourable results, it has no spiritual merit. Good must be good for itself and not for the praise you get out of it. It is better to give pennies away from public eyes than pounds with your name appearing.

What are the chief morals? Love comes in the first place, and, if of divine quality, all the rest goes with it.

If love is biased, then you will see that the other attributes also weaken. You may say that there are people who never told a lie, but cannot truly love, and the former attribute is a great merit, but we tell you that anybody who says that he never lied is lying when he says so. Others, having lived in a life of charity again without love, receive no merit because if you give as a duty not accompanied by love, most of the good is lost. A farthing handed with love is worth more than a thousand pounds of money given for duty.

You are doing wrong by exclamations concerning an individual if you have no concrete knowledge as to the justification of such an exclamation. Even if you have proof, it is better to abstain from gossip as it so easily oversteps barriers, and by the time it reaches the third person, it is completely changed from the original. We also refer to unduly praise, though that of course is far less harmful and most ridicules the person who said it. By gossip, you gain nothing, and at the same instant, you lower your own soul. You can never defend enough. How do you know that you are better?

Those who gossip are the enemies of God. Justness must be the light on Earth.

We beg you to never to speak ill of anyone, unless you have certain proof and then only to teach others. You can say that you avoid some individuals, but do not gossip about them. You can rebuke those who gossip, but you must never start a gossip.

The only pure souls are those who can give with a loving heart even to those who wish them ill.

Love

If you have true love, you can never sin greatly, but if a person rejects and measures love and belief, you can never know what the individual in question might do.

Try to nurse only love in you even for those who annoy you. Start when you wake in the morning. Know that every ill thought turns you away from God. Remember that the true religion of God is love. If you start your day with only love in your thoughts, you will come in direct contact with God.

For us, the essential regarding a soul is how much love he possesses because on that depends how you build up your work.

Man knows so little of the importance of spontaneous emotions of love and their help through the waves they send all along the spheres, but we repeat the emotions must be spontaneous or else they are of no value to us up here. One must aim at reaching perfection through spontaneousity. The Great One, although law and order in Himself, is the symbol of spontaneousity. That is why everything He creates has a beauty man can never attain. Love must always be spontaneous and unexpected. We would like to speak of the importance of spontaneous good and charitable acts.

Whenever that impulse overtakes you, do not reject it, but act immediately, no matter what the cause was or is. Those sudden gushes of impulses come to you from very high regions and are, therefore, so swift, as the higher you dwell, the quicker the waves move because they wish to touch multitudes. Very few realise the importance and greatness of those sudden impulses. Evil never stops working in exactly the opposite direction, though the waves are slow and of another quality.

Some souls have created a god to their liking and cannot submit to the law of love and obedience, which are inseparable. Love, respect, and the law of unconditional obedience are of one and the same family. This is our rule, not by force, but because it is the truth, and the truth has no sideshows.

Goodness is wise, but never weak. If it is weak, it cannot be absolute goodness.

You must be firm towards the wrongdoer or else you are not the child of pure love, which is God. Those possessed with envy, jealousy, malice, and self-love are the enemies of God, so how can we just look at them—or worse—use gentle words to them? No, firmness is correct. What you must not do is to wish ill to anyone, not even the worst criminal.

If love forms your life, no ill will can enter your heart, and if there is no ill will, you need no laws. If men are told that the law is in themselves, they would think more deeply and be filled with self-respect, not avoiding to do harm only for fear of the law. If it was revealed from your childhood that all law is in you there would be peace on Earth because only a few would then want to break the law.

If one possesses true self-respect, one must respect the neighbour, and if you respect your neighbour, you will wish him well and if you wish him well, there is no need of a law that forbids you to take away the cow or the land or any of your neighbour's belongings.

Happiness

Try to be always bright and gay. Even your bodily vigour depends on that. Moods, glooms and such things have ill effects on one's body, as they draw bad waves.

We like you to be serious in your work, but little frivolities are not to be excluded. The main thing in one's earthly and daily life is to keep under a balanced control. Serious work can be carried on in the same way. Use all in harmony and temperance, and no trouble will touch you.

Too much seriousness is not always good. There are moments in life when seriousness is unavoidable; yet earnestness is a better word. As long as one is not serious about one's own importance, all is well, but to take oneself too much in earnest is ridiculous and against the humbleness which is the mirror of God's light in us.

Your so varied moods will not do. You must learn to live in greater contentment and so draw to yourselves waves of the same order. Remember that like attracts like. You must also acquire an attitude of positiveness. You are too easily influenced by immediate surroundings.

We wish to tell you that the Great One is the originator of humour, and it is a great mistake to make things too solemn.

What is solemnity, if you reflect? Its fundamental lies in an egotic atmosphere, a kind of self-importance, self-administration, and you know who is the originator of the latter. Humour, if truly free from vulgarity, is the cleanest of all things to possess and it shows the humane impression of oneself. Christ was a great humorist, but mankind could not understand such subtleness and misrepresented most of His gaiety for solemn importance.

Go about with a happy smile. It will make others smile. Have some divertimento. You must feed your soul with a great deal of beauty and variance. Be serious but also gay and jolly.

Avoid your ill-willers, but do not talk about them, lest you become the same. Do not ever reject those who love you. That is a stab straight into God.

Cheerfulness brings good conditions and quicker because gloom and sadness are unknown in the very highest spheres and likely to cast a mist on your waves, which you must try to avoid.

The waves of sorrow and unhappiness do not reach up. They only mar the free flow of the waves carrying harmonious conditions.

Joy must be in your hearts. We try to convince mankind of the importance of a joyful state of mind.

Sorrow brings sorrow. Joy brings joy. Onwards you win; look back and you lose. Unless what you call your amusements are under a controlled moderation, you are lost for a spiritual life and have to return somewhere until you realise on your own that it is so.

Be always clean in your body. You would not like to keep a diamond in a dirty case, especially if you know that you can never take it out.

Balance

A quality you can make growing in yourselves is the attitude of satisfaction and balance in your judgments. To acquire a quiet, calm attitude of mind is also to be practiced. It is in real peace of the wave flow you receive true spiritual visions. We never hurry and, thus, the inflow of wisdom penetrates into us and leaves its root.

Men who cannot stick to their work and constantly wish for a change prove thereby their unsettled and unbalanced soul condition, and it becomes extremely difficult for us to help them with success as the wave conditions of a person must be held in perfect order.

What is self-control? Let us analyse it. It is a wish to show up a different nature to the real one. Now let us see where we stand. If you, for example, feel a great anger for a fellow man and if you are what you call on Earth a decent person, you will control your anger and so believe yourself to be a wonderful fellow for doing it. Where is your wonderfulness in controlling an anger, a grievance if that results in a lifelong hatred and grudge, perhaps, for that person in whose favour you exercise control? The grudge you will carry on with you will do continual harm as, you know by now, that the waves of words unsaid do harm. Better have it out before thousand eyes and clear it up than to keep your thoughts seen by the one eye, who sees everything, though you do not quite trust that.

Do you see the uselessness in this respect?

Let us now go further and examine what the use of self-control with regard to love means. Of course, we mean true love and not lust. How often soul-mates have missed reunion by their controlling feelings which they are not sure will be reciprocated by the other. Many disasters have been caused by such self-control, which may be attributed to nothing else than your vanity, controlling your true self.

Self-control is noble and necessary when you are certain that only your own person is the loser and you, without any vindictive feelings or self-admiration, are able to make the sacrifice. For instance, if you are ill, and you see your beloved worrying around you, it is noble to feign that you are not suffering greatly.

Truly, to control your desires when your own self is solely concerned is the right thing and certainly the one which gradually shall kill the influence of evil, because, as we told you, desires are the curse of evil.

Have you thought that life itself never changed its speed? A child cannot and will not grow up quicker than the heavenly mathematics have decided. Have you seen flowers grow up in speed? No, were they to do so, they would destroy themselves. It is dangerous for earthly souls to wish *for the acquirement of the speed of the spirits, who can be and are everywhere simultaneously. That is possible without the flesh, but soul-killing with flesh.*

If the soul constantly is in a hurry, it cannot develop its qualities and capacity of visions. Cannot man grasp that it is evil driving you like in a fury, not allowing quiet thoughts to rule, thoughts that may open your souls to the real visions which still are buried in you.

Humbleness reflects God in your expressions and gives you new light, lifting you to a higher realm of thoughts already whilst on Earth. It is not for you to speak of your merits, but for others to see them and for you then to raise higher. Each of you must be very severe judges of your own improvement, but nevertheless keep the right balance.

Deception

Nothing is more deplorable than a hypocrite as he deceives on Earth and stains his soul. It is perhaps one of the most difficult things for the hypocrite to see light on his arrival up here as his own falsehood overshadows even the little light he carries with himself.

There are three graduations of lies. The first one is harmful to a high degree to your fellow man; the second harmful to yourself and the last is the lie which averts trouble and, therefore, harmless in all respects.

Let us see what we consider a lie which harms others. If you, for example, wish to obtain a position or anything else which belongs to someone, no matter whether the individual in question deserves to have it or not, if you, as we say, try through lies, invented by yourself to make that person lose what he holds, it is a serious sin and there is no doubt that you have allowed evil to guide you. It will take a long time to purify yourself after you have left Earth unless you repent and admit the wrong you have done and you so deny evil's power.

Now we come to the lies which only harm yourself. They are the ones which lower your existence, marring your improvement. Such lies are, for example boasting of your achievements and making your friends believe something about you which you are not. Those lies are minor things, yet you will feel humiliated once you come up here.

Now as to lies of avoiding unpleasantness. As long as they are limited to that purpose, do not involve complications, and do settle disagreements, they are regarded as a necessity. If you, for instance, know that a disaster is approaching a person and can by a lie avert it, you are entitled to say the lie, which will be understood up here, because if you would tell that person that something horrible would befall him and he does not believe you, he would turn against you. In reality, you are doing the correct thing, although it needed a lie which humans would condemn, knowing so little.

Never lie if you do harm with it, were it even to a fly, but to keep peace a lie is permissible. Do not, however, think that any lies are a merit. Lies are forgiven if said for the sake of helping.

We also know how hard it is in life to control your thoughts and not lie with them, but one can improve in that respect greatly.

Tact

We never spoke of tact. Tact is a difficult attribute to acquire and unless it is inborn or rather carried with you from your spirit life, it can easily become a hypocritical attitude.

What is tact exactly? It is a noble and sublime characteristic of a high developed soul. In what way does it show itself? You would say that it is demonstrated by a person who chooses his words well and is careful in what he says, lest people should be hurt or offended. That is your idea of tact, isn't it? Here you make a great mistake, forgetting altogether that it is your thoughts that count. You may have intended to convey just the opposite to what you carefully put into tactful words, thus creating waves to evil's liking, lowering the pictures which are registered up here and showing your real nature.

That kind of attitude is not tact, but falsehood.

On the other hand, if you have a true loving heart and soul, you possess the true kind of tact, which goes with it. If you have something painful to report, you will not choose words which are diplomatic, but you will lovingly explain even the worst. You cannot disturb people if you are true in your love for mankind. Your consideration for them will be a part of you. You will not either interfere with their affairs, love knowing that the affairs of others do not concern yourself.

You have a very good proverb in England and that is: 'Mind your own business.' If that was used in general, we assure you that lots of trouble on Earth would never take place. Curiosity with regard to finding out facts concerning people for malicious reasons or for lust of sheer mischief and used for slander falls under the rules of sinning.

Never criticise so as not to be criticised. Remember that although your neighbour may not share your views, his may not be inferior to yours.

What you on Earth will never understand is that you are judged by your thoughts up here, and that your whole future existence will be and is built up by them. Man must learn this for his improvement.

Be careful that your thoughts should not be different from your talk, even if it involves rudeness.

Refinement of words, of thoughts, of actions—that is what man must learn and that will become the first step towards the destruction of evil.

Advance in refinement, in subtle feelings, grow in love, but never mind if you do not get it returned. Silence towards those who understand you not. Talks and explanations are worse than spirit sprayed on fire.

There is a great deal to be said for those who say little but think profoundly.

One must be short but straight, and fear is altogether out of the question. Either you are in the wrong and you admit it, or you are right and then there is only one route and that is the direct one. Only evil uses indirect routes. You must be wise in your tolerance and not give a wreath to the undeserving.

Vulgarity

We should like to emphasise the importance of soul elevation and the practice of a state of mind, which gradually loses all traces of vulgarity. On Earth, vulgarity at present is occupying a very prominent place. We see, however, that a flicker of revelation appears in the thought of man which indicates an awakening to this fact and our request is urgent that man should fully realise the repulsiveness of that attitude.

Lead a healthy life. Never be abusive of material which are for the improvement of the body. Drink and eat moderately. Excess of both numbs the soul and gives chances to evil for using the body for evil purposes.

Nothing is more repellent to us in the world of the spirits, nothing more harmful to humans than all the drinking which is taking place, especially among the youth. Just think to what they are building up the frame which was created for their soul's purification. How can the soiled body wash its soul from blemishes?

You can also be vulgar without seeming so in action, which is almost worse, because the waves of the invisible are more powerful than those of the visible. You can, however, soon discover a vulgar mind as the expression of the individuals so possessed gets uglier as they get older.

Vulgarity is an ugly sin, especially if done by persons of education, and yet you will find it more amongst the rich than amongst the poor. Why? Because money urges you to become vulgar. It tempts mankind to all sorts of vices, pushes them to show off and prevents the development of the soul.

Society Life

Many of us were tempted when on Earth to attend glittering functions. Now we see what we wasted, and many of us have regretted to see the pictures which no one escapes seeing when arriving up here. Nothing is more pitiful and shameful than to see the pictures in which the souls show up their self-importance.

It is not what you seem to be in the eyes of the world, but what you are inwardly that makes you a superior spirit.

It is sad to see how you waste your days by superficial parties. Nothing in it. They do not even ask you for the sake of love or sympathy. They may even hate [someone], but if it makes their function [grander] they do not care. Falsehood fails like all bad things. They go to houses afterwards, abusing and laughing at one and yet the host and hostess believed it a great success. They become a pitiful picture.

Brotherhood is crying out for a re-establishment of life on Earth. Society life leads to nothing. The hours one wastes in the company of society, one could use in contemplating alone in one's own room and harken to the inner voices or our waves, better expressed. You would then advance a great deal faster.

One must stand by oneself when one is in the company of the insincere. If you want to rise, if you want to live in divine love, you must resign earthly glitters and ignore the ill tongues, who will always fall on true seekers.

Praise on Earth or fame does not count up here. Only unselfish love and a spiritual rise have any value to us.

We wish you to be gay, jolly, and enjoy life's fine things in music, pictures, and the company of good souls, but to keep away from the artificial kind of people who have no real feeling for anything deep, but go about Earth like parrots, imitating their neighbours.

Evil wants people to indulge in so-called amusements, but in reality, the more you seek amusement, the more you yearn for something you cannot explain. Up here, there is constant work and that is what makes spirit life so wonderful and such an exhilarating bliss.

Friendship

You are each of you a living magnet, and just like a magnet, you can only draw that which is allied with itself.

On Earth, there are many stages and everyone draws to his or her likes. When you meet a person and that person is in harmony with you, you will feel the unmistakable current of the same kind of waves as your own touching you. If that happens and you later on change your mind you are a bad judge, as then you judge with your brain which often misguides you. Once you feel that you truly love a person, it becomes a bad judgment if, say, someone points out faults or inspires distrust against him [and] you begin to hesitate through the impression of the influence you were exposed to. Besides, minor faults must not and ought not to lessen friendship, once it has really become friendship. It ought, on the contrary, to make you wish to be of use and to help his defects. The chief thing is on no account to judge anyone, unless you have concrete proofs for believing this or that.

Good judgment consists in being able to see whether a person is unbiased or whether he keeps his word and does not change his moods or is continually contradicting his previous attitude. Therefore, we say that you must watch for yourself and follow your own feelings.

If you should discover that you love a person for material benefit and not for the sake of pure friendship, do not become intimate with such a person, as you are sure to get into disharmony [with this person] sooner or later and you, thus, create enemies and help evil.

If man would go after his instinct, which is the wave, the voice of his guardian spirit, there would not be all the mischief and wickedness done that there is.

One must never judge from anybody's but one's own self, as each individual is a separate personality, some more, some less developed, but distinctly an individual with his own soul and his own waves. It is decidedly wrong to judge from the point of view of someone else. If you, for example, truly like a person, but get biased by a third one declaring that you err and that the person is unworthy of your love, you are making a great mistake and your judgment is nil altogether. Through your wavering, you create disturbing waves, harming the desire of establishing harmony amongst souls on Earth.

Never, though, give too quick a judgment unless you know unmistakably that you are entitled to judge as you did.

Supposing there is a doubt in your heart concerning a person, and you do not tell that person what you feel about him, you will then start concealing facts and from that unnatural situations arise and the doubts in you will accumulate and many new imaginative thoughts will enter you and so the loved person will in the end become an alien. If you instead would truthfully admit ugly feelings, they will be cleared up, leaving no traces behind. Vice breeds vice rapidly; evil is always ready to urge you against goodness. The way people talk on Earth they show clearly that they are absolutely ignorant concerning their own ego. Were they to study themselves, they would soon find that they possess all the faults attributed to their neighbour and that in their very own self.

Be more tolerant. When you judge, ask yourself first whether you have not done the same; or put yourself in the state of others, then judge.

All of you on Earth attach such an importance to what people say. Some of you even regulate your lives wholly according to that, but few among you listen to what the voices say within you and yet that is the voice you shall meet up here and you will feel a stranger before it. That voice comes through spiritual channels to you, and the source is the Great One.

If you ignore attacks, you do not draw any bad influences, whilst if you dwell on unpleasant things, persons, or objects, you create conditions for bad influences to surround you.

It is an astonishing fact that a soul under evil influences senses fear on behalf the other person towards him or her quicker than anything else and uses that as a powerful weapon. Only when fear is absent are you the master of the situation.

Beauty

Look at all the beauty of a flowering tree, look at the gentle flow of a pure river which mirrors your image and reflects the rays of God–yet men hesitate in the certainty of Him. You find God everywhere, yet you look for Him. Believe this, dormant souls, and you will see that happiness is not on your doorstep, but in your very hearts. Once you feel that, you become the richest man on Earth, as you, thus, receive a part of the heavenly treasures.

What is beauty on Earth? The relics of former times, the sceneries of various countries, the art of great sculptors, the works of old masters, some entertainments, especially where the lines of the body display a harmonical beauty, the growth of flowers, the life in the jungle, the setting of the sun, the movement of the seas, a display of master skating, in fact everything where poise and strength are combined, and the greatest of all the embrace of true mates in harmony and peace. God presented so much on Earth which can give you great joy, provided it is held constantly in a true balance.

If souls on Earth would live in beauty and understanding, they would become better as those attributes bring or rather draw good towards them.

It is those who always work against aesthetics, against godliness, who bring evil into more power.

You must realise more strongly how much of beauty there is in your lives and, in fact, on Earth. If you should live in gloom, you cannot but continue in the same way after you left Earth. It is very much according to *how you live and think on Earth that you shall continue up here, which after all must be logical to you.*

The more you dwell on beauty and spiritual emotions, the greater the beauty of expression becomes. Your eyes are the mirror of the soul, and you will often notice as you advance on Earth that they lose all their beauty. No one under the influence of evil can hide that which reveals the true picture of the soul's nature.

Lead a life full of love and kindness, live also in various kinds of art and nurse tolerance towards your neighbour. Forgive those who wish you harm. Remember that God is the light in your hearts, and reveal that to mankind. Then your lives will not differ greatly from what you shall find up here in the first states, and you cannot either go far wrong in your life on Earth.

One must already on Earth train oneself to a great range of variety in interests. It will more resemble the life which awaits you. Can you imagine the Great One limited? No, you say. Very well, then you know that you are born out of His spark, so use out every interest in you, spread it, nurse it, study, and you will never feel downhearted. Only idleness of thought causes moods, unknown to the high world of the spirits. We see this so clearly in the waves shooting out in the universe, and many definitely justify our statement. Try not to waste the gold which is in you. Polish it up till its shine gives you perfect peace and the real beauty of an inner life.

Let men worry you, let them laugh, and sneer at you. Even if you know that you are in rags, the Great One whose light you allowed to shine through you will keep your spirit clad in gold.

Positiveness

Is there any greater contrast than light and darkness? With the former you see clearer as days pass by, whilst in darkness you get daily blinder.

It is better to see things in black and white than to hesitate, as it is always a merit to admit a mistake, if it happens, than to have an undecided opinion of humans.

Courage is the defeat of evil, provided it is used wisely and knows where to stop. The balance and the harmony are equally needed in courage as in any other enterprise.

It is better for the speeding of wishes to take up an attitude of certainty. This is a rule with spirit life. These things are difficult to understand, but it is a sure fact.

If you can wish absolutely unbiased, all obstacles are sooner defeated. Drive away thoughts of hesitation of all kind. Be positive in your actions and always demand your rights. Up here, the word hesitation is finished; therefore we go steadily ahead. If you wish your waves to reach a destination, you can only succeed if your feeling is of a decisive nature. If one has a variation of feelings concerning a thing, the waves will get entangled, confused, muddled, and, finally, because of lack of strength, dissolve in the embrace of powerful waves. A soul of inspired visions must be without wavering in his emotions and feelings and never for a second hesitate to speak out as long as he is convinced in his feelings. Souls must always be positive. Negative emotions are lies and a deceit to your ego.

Make your plans and believe in them and, thus, you draw them towards you. Everything can be attained in this way, but time must of course not worry you as then you make your wishes follow earthly laws, and the spiritual waves weaken. Those who build a castle in their inner thoughts get it ultimately. The best explanation is that by firm trust, you are brought to meet the corresponding waves and, as we told you, mankind magnetically receives what it sends out.

What you, man on Earth, has not grasped yet is that anything emanating from you finds corresponding waves and shall ultimately return to you and that much more powerfully, as it carries with it its double.

Accept the fact that to have perseverance and patience is a part of the Great One, and you ought to delight in difficulties and problems which are, we tell you, surmountable if you practise the attitude just mentioned.

Very often, arguments push aside immediate events. Therefore, arguments are dangerous undertakings, as you never know which are the ones you harm by such a practice. We are fully aware of how hard it is on Earth to accommodate to and meet spirit conditions, and that is why so many things are delayed and some events even missed altogether. You must understand the importance of keeping a straight and clear line which shoots out corresponding wave vibrations. Only those can reach high up unhindered. What you need, all of you, is enthusiasm—yes, enthusiasm for all the beauty which is within you.

Enthusiasm comes from the divine source, and if you dwell on it, you approach the circle of the Great One.

One must be wise and overcome small matters and worries in an effortless way. The soul who sees the outline of problems always succeeds in entering the whole ultimately, so have as your motto: 'Do not worry, but act wisely!'

It is the big lines which you possess which count in your life. The small things must not bother you, especially when you know that it is what evil wishes.

The motive which leads you to us is the simplest, yet the most difficult to attain. It is love, and love has no side roads. It is either there, or it is not. Life, down there with you, just as up here with us, must be and is either one thing or another. It cannot waver. Any hesitation acts disturbingly, thus creating a definite confusion in the flow of waves.

All your great souls were positive in their movements, actions, and beliefs. Great men cannot have several points of view. You must be absolutely certain that you know what you want and never question yourself as to its being right or wrong if you are a good and loving soul, as then you must be certain that what you wish for is the only right thing and then you win. If you begin to analyse, you lose your battle, you can be sure.

If you are wise, you know the things to avoid. Therefore, fear is unnecessary.

What we are keen for you to learn and acquire is the courage of speaking out the truth and never, never [avoid] it or robe it in clothes of sham material.

If you reflect, you must realise that the greatest on Earth is how much courage you have in saying out your thoughts exactly and in the most truthful manner. How few of you do it and yet it builds up your whole future spirit existence. Why do you think that you have been given the use of your free will, if not for developing your purity? Up here, every camouflage of truth becomes a muddle in your picture and makes for a standstill. By avoiding the direct truth, you bring such shadows upon yourselves that you immediately give scope for evil's power, taking joy in playing with the shadows.

Prayer

Pray daily for a constant communion with God. Do not try to imagine Him. You cannot. Love His warmth, and that is enough. When your thoughts are filled with love and you forget yourselves, it happens that you meet directly with the light of the Great One and only that can give you the happiness which is disconnected from Earth. Little private talks to the Great One are the only ones that reach Him straight, because of their childish nature. Verily, we say that except for those who can be children, it will be difficult to enter the sphere of light.

Why can you not pray at home or out in the open under the mantle of the spirits? Do you think that God comes near you when you are bored in your hearts or feel disgust for those who embrace a different faith to the one you possess? Prayers of spiritual inspiration are not put on a tray like a piece of mutton for the glut of everyone. Real prayer is the flow from the spirit and the one thing you cannot talk about, as its vibrations are the confessions of the individual soul with God.

Never look down when you pray. Look up into the universe, up to the sky. You must not feel ashamed when you talk to God. He is so above all that you can imagine that shame or fear would not be understood by Him. You must not pray for ambitious wants or earthly success. That is unknown to God. Remember that thoughts count up here. If you pray in solitude for hours, but with the intention of defeating something or someone, your prayers become associated with evil. Only purity can send waves which reach the high spheres.

Prayers do not on all occasions reach the Great One, which ought to be easy to understand. Remember that scores of people pray for the destruction of others or for personal greed. Those, of course, never reach God, as it was the waves of evil that gave them the yearning for evil things.

How can you imagine that a prayer for someone's success or any such thing would reach God? To us, it sounds so careless and disrespectful towards God. Only prayers of pure love can reach God and prayers of a selfless kind. Do your work properly and do it hard, then you get your own perseverance rewarded. God can only help your spiritual improvement. The waves which reach high up are waves combined of goodness and pure conviction. If such, they travel higher and higher and reach to

God. This does not, however, happen very frequently, as few on Earth can have unbiased thoughts and wishes.

The waves with ill wishes never reach up. They, however, find a home where low spirits dwell and there the schemes do wrong for man on Earth.

There are waves of hesitation. They vanish as they are too weak to continue. It may be that they meet with others of a less hesitative nature and, joining them, reach a higher sphere.

There are waves of yearning souls wandering along the universe, but not reaching the truth. If you have a great wish, and the waves try to penetrate through the spheres, they can only do so if no other waves are interfering. All this ought to show to you how many obstacles there are for the waves to pass through.

People go to church and pray, yet are unprepared to do any sacrifice and leave to the mercy of God those less fortunate than themselves. They make God their servant, and believe us, there is a number of such people who expect from God what they would think degrading for themselves to do.

Indeed, there is a need for man to realise that unless they grasp that God is in them, and they use that power, God cannot descend where He is already.

If a prayer is coming from your heart and is purely spiritual, or has a wish connected with similar motives, it invariably reaches the Great One or at least His highest messenger.

The prayers which are earnest, yet too much material, get dispersed and never reach the highest spheres.

The best is if you ask the Great One to do as He wishes, as He knows what is best for you ultimately.

We continually see in the thoughts of man, notice in their acts, that they appeal to God and even expect the Great One to do the work for them. Do men on Earth not realise that work is life and doubly so when the flesh has been left behind? The whole calculation of heavenly mathematics is an eternal work of what man tries but can never reach, a motion which is perpetual.

The work of the Great One is such that it cannot be grasped by mankind. The greatest man on Earth with the utmost capacity for work is less when compared to the Great One than an invisible screw in the giant machinery. All on Earth is a preparation for the real great work that is awaiting you on your arrival up here. We and you must work to destroy evil, so that light can shine on the souls and Earth may become one of the recreations for spirits living in space.

You know that you have to undergo the state of purgatory on Earth and why not make it as beautiful as possible? Why spoil that which is likeable in it constantly through lamenting for a future life? You know that you have to go through it, so do it bravely, not omitting the fact that you were sent down for purification, and purification cannot take place if your soul is filled with pessimism.

If the world would love—if envy, malice, greed, vengeance, hatred, lust for the sake of lust, were completely destroyed in the hearts of men—then glory would descend to Earth and take you upon golden wings to where you and we all belong.

The spirit messengers do not waiver in their assertion that advancement is our personal task. The strengthening of the free will for choosing good, and the gradual development of individual qualities in the fight against evil, lies in our own hands or the progress we make would simply become mechanical and lose its spiritual value.

We are told:

It is impossible for the true soul to become mechanical, as the waves which are yourselves are ever varying just as with Him, Who kissed the spirit of each of you, is a continual variation.

Life must grow from within and our fate is shaped by ourselves. Each individual stands alone, listening to the guidance poured into their soul, freely building and decorating the mansion they wish to enter on their return to the world of reality.

16

FINAL REFLECTIONS

Having read the messages, the reader may be asking, "Can I believe that these communications really came from the disembodied residents of the afterworld?" To those unversed in extra-sensory or paranormal events, this is a valid question. For those who have long been involved in the search for truths concerning life, death and God, the substance of the messages itself is confirmation that a higher wisdom was present and delivering the communications.

According to the receivers' notes, there was concern with the issue of proof of the validity of the transcribed messages and their source. The subject was addressed by the messengers who believed that publication of "proofs" would be self-defeating of the information they seek to disseminate. According to the records of the group receiving the messages, certain tests were performed to authenticate the source of this information. The experiments challenged the messengers to provide information or facts on remote events or of individuals' private thoughts known only to the members. The messengers reluctantly participated and removed any member's doubt as to their authenticity. However, the spirits were adamantly opposed to the publishing of these tests to convince skeptics. As to their position and reasoning for avoiding proofs, the messengers stated that the following be placed in any public exposure of their work:

The lines of showing proofs we do not approve of. You must not excuse your work. It has to be believed on its own merit and value, or they must leave it. Any sign of eagerness to show proofs of its authenticity reveals weakness and even remote doubting in oneself. Say what you feel regarding the method, the working, the corrections, the tacit system, but no references to any of these incidents showing proofs. The instant you trust because of proofs, your trust has no value and cannot reach any spiritual upheaval, nor come into contact with the high waves and with His light.

The revelations must stand on their own and vibrate through their strength. We want you to present this message as we give it to you.

We are instructed to reveal to the world that earthly life can have great beauty to all, but that no one can avoid some sorrow or trouble or misery, because Earth is not the dwelling of absolute purity and the souls on their own drifted from that purity. They must remember, however, that, as we said, there is much beauty on Earth, and if they realise this, they come closer to what they once were. But refrain from demonstrating proofs. Truth is alone and must so continue or else it is not truth. Nothing is real if it needs comparation. We cannot emphasise enough how vital it is to trust in a pure trusting.

What we object to and definitely repulse is curiosity and the wish to explain everything through and with your perishable brain. It is in every case a drifting again from the Great One, ergo renewed sinnings and why? Because you do not want to admit nor allow that only God knows everything, and then everything too which is bound with love and light, the two combined giving perfect love.

We are speaking from His light up here to His light in every soul on Earth. When these lights meet and realise they have met, then redemption will start and love dominate where greed, envy, and hatred is being nursed.

Should a reader of these messages want to believe but is afraid that that belief is unreasonable or irrational, it may help to acknowledge that the subject has, after all, been examined and contemplated for millennia. If you choose to believe the messengers and their promise of eternal life, you are in good company. Many religious and philosophical thinkers over the ages acknowledge these truths. Of course, the major religions all base their precepts on the eternal soul.

Plato (Socrates), Aristotle, Marcus Aurelius, Maimonides, Avicenna, St. Thomas Aquinas, St. Augustine, Descartes, Kierkegaard, and such transcendentalists as March, Henry, Hedge, Emerson, and Schweitzer are all in accord with the messengers' testimony.

Marcus Aurelius believed in the divine quality of the soul, as a part of God temporarily inhabiting the body of man.

St. Thomas Aquinas leaves no doubt as to his conviction of the duality of spirit and body and the immortality of the soul.

René Descartes, in his psychophysical parallelism, describes God's synchronization of soul and body, the former surviving the latter.

Kierkegaard's philosophy of religion is completely Christian, in regard to God, soul, and immortality.

Many outstanding contemporary thinkers have expressed themselves on the survival of the spirit: Arthur H. Compton, physicist: "I prefer to believe he lives on after death, continuing in a larger sphere, in co-operation with his Maker, the work he had here begun."

Howell Hart of Duke University, referring to Dr. Rhine's research on ESP: "That our consciousness can observe and operate apart from the physical brain and body encourages my beliefs in the soul that transcends the body... the event called 'death' in our earthly lives can be but an episode in the far vaster adventure. Religion has been telling us that for ages."

Evidently, many on Earth are coming to similar conclusions, as the messengers acknowledge:

> Souls are awakening to the knowledge of an infinite power and wish to open up to allow that power to flow in. There are innumerable souls who now are trying to come into contact with us and who realise the importance of the various waves. Hitherto we could not succeed in using that power, but now it is the event of all thinking souls.

We are evolving at a faster pace and must be alert to the signs of guidance.

On the subject of doubt, that beings from another sphere can communicate spiritual truths to those on Earth, it is worthwhile to note the following interchange with the messengers on the issue of skepticism. Just above, the spirits talked of an increased awareness in mankind for just such contact. As we become higher evolved, we seek higher truths. This raised the question of why the musical geniuses, mentioned in an earlier chapter, descended with their heavenly gifts later than the scientific and mathematical messengers.

Why is it so difficult to entertain the idea that communications between the visible and the invisible worlds take place? Do we not already feel that the veil has become very transparent? In the history of religions, we discern a progress culminating in the coming of Christ; the history of art shows a similar tendency. The arrival of musical compositions by Bach, Mozart, Beethoven, and others, bringing patterns of divine beauty to Earth, came late in the day. Advanced beings appear when we are ready to accept them. "When the student is ready, the teacher will appear..." – Lao Tzu

The messengers addressed the timing of our enlightenment by stating:

> Why is music the last of all? Music is so high up here that man needed great knowledge of all other arts to understand that it combines both immediate touch with God and with architecture, sculpture, painting and poetry. Only after mankind had received true illumination from the previous arts was it decided by various messengers to descend and give mankind some of the sound of divinity. Hence the long interval before the great ones descended to Earth, revealing a new delight to starving souls. Music is love, charity and the light of God.

If there is a plan and meaning in human life, it is not unreasonable that we become more closely acquainted with it as centuries pass by. Humans' spiritual growth through reincarnation and heightened awareness eventually approaches a level which allows us to take notice. A definition of life is growth, and life does not exist where stagnation or decline prevails. Changes must be and are taking place. We are at the forefront of an emergent evolution, bringing new truths and perspectives into acceptance which in turn impel us to reconsider our priorities. The pessimists are wrong. We see growth and "new things under the sun" continually appear.

In support of our purpose our spirit friends say:

You know that you are a spark of God, and if you feel that, you imme-diately draw God in you and are capable of doing what you never dreamt of being able to achieve, but how many of you realise that truth?

Man's spirit emerges from obscurity and moves toward a place in the light, acting in close communion with all those who draw towards the Source of eternal light. The calling is for eternity.

There is no end in the world of reality. Perfection has no limit. On Earth you seem to think that a standstill occurs at the wall raised by your con-ception of a perfect state. This comes from your mechanical outlook. A material thing having received a perfect shape and finish you cannot better it according to your views, but art may bring you to a clearer idea. The true artist leaves a work he thinks perfect, as he cannot do better at the moment, but feels that it may become perfected.

This is the nearest explanation we can give as to what perfectioning of perfection means in a spiritual sense.

Assurance for Our Future

It is clear after reading the messages that there is a refreshing joyfulness and carefree optimism emanating from the spirits. The whole atmos-phere becomes vibrant with cheerfulness and trust. Bliss without so-lemnity, contentment in activity, enjoyment free of guilt, love that never tires—the natural emotional state in their blessed realm. A new arrival from Earth must be happily surprised, as the spirit companions continually underscore their joyous dominion:

Be merry, that is what we like and ask for. Great solemnity becomes ridiculous and does not exist up here except in prayer. You have no idea how jolly we are up here, and the higher, the gayer we are. How could it be otherwise considering that His light sparkles around us?

But no happiness could possibly endure either in the high regions or on Earth if suffering and evil were to persist. Those in the light, who know that dwellers in darkness exist, could never enjoy complete bliss until they knew that ultimate restoration, individual and universal, was approaching. But we are told that is on the way:

In the essence of your being, you are all good, as the Great One could not create evil. Your soul resembles the sun. At times it is covered by clouds interfering with its warmth and healing power, sometimes even enveloping it to almost complete darkness, but remember the sun is still there underneath, intact and pure. So it is with the soul. Evil is the cloud, but the day shall arrive when those clouds will disperse for eternity and His light shine through all and everything.

Only perfect good is eternal. If you realise that your life is eternal, you more easily understand that good is all power, as gradually all will return to His light which is everlasting.

The final stage of individual advance is absolute purification until you reach the spheres, where only love and light exist and where you lose yourself in it with a glory man cannot understand.

Evil itself will perish:

It is perishable except for the spark which is from God and though it never developed cannot be annihilated. Evil has some of God's light and, therefore, hope is never lost that the light of God will one day come to the fore and so the universe will shine without shadows. All lost spirits will ultimately return to Him.

An anticipation of that event was earlier mentioned in connection with the declaration that God knows no evil and that, consequently, evil is perishable and has an end. But the positive assurance that a spark of the divine is alive, though hidden, even in the midst of deepest darkness, confirms that hope and inspires a firm trust in the restoration of all things.

As we say farewell to our Friends of the Light for now, they leave us with this closing certainty:

Mankind will be saved by his own conviction that pure love is God, and pure love means sharing everything and living in joy, knowing truly that the waves of spirits are joined to Earth so that the two worlds will unite into one.

ABOUT THE AUTHORS

Reginald H. Gray

Reginald's belief developed over many years of studying metaphysical and spiritual writings and from his own paranormal experiences and contact from his guardian spirit. On more than one occasion, in his youth, his life was saved by the intervention of an invisible protector.

Years later, when his two sons, ages two and six at the time, were snatched by their mother against court orders and taken to a foreign country under false names, he was able to locate them by paranormal means.

Reginald Gray has written in the alternative health and legal fields, as well as a treatise on the life of Royal Rife, who claimed to have discovered a cure for cancer in the 1940s. He is presently working on a novel based on the spiritual principles and truths found in *Messages from Beyond the Veil: Spiritual Guidance for Our Human Experience*.

David J. Dye

David's parents instilled in him at a young age a grand wonder about the nature of the universe and the purpose of existence, a love of science and science-fiction, and a belief that anything is possible.

David carries this curiosity with him into his professional pursuits, which include ghostwriting and editing books in topics ranging from Greek mythology to American history, and developing curriculum in spiritualism, intuitive studies, mindfulness, holistic nutrition, and more.

CPSIA information can be obtained
at www.ICGtesting.com
Printed in the USA
BVHW031321170821
614621BV00005B/58